Modern
Waterfowl
Hunting

Modern Waterfowl Hunting

Hunter's Information Series ®
North American Hunting Club
Minneapolis, Minnesota

Modern Waterfowl Hunting

Copyright © 1987, North American Hunting Club

Library of Congress Catalog Card Number 87-061016
ISBN 0-914697-09-9

Printed in U.S.A.
    3   4   5   6   7   8   9

Caution

Contents

Acknowledgments

This book is the successful result of contributions from many sources. Foremost, these include author Monte Burch, NAHC Managing Editor Bill Miller, NAHC Associate Editor Steve Pennaz, NAHC Member Projects Manager Mike Vail and his assistant Valarie Waldron.

Ducks Unlimited has also made a special contribution to *Modern Waterfowl Hunting* by providing the color illustrations from their field guide. On behalf of the North American Hunting Club we give heartfelt congratulations to DU on its 50th Anniversary.

Mark LaBarbera
Executive Vice President
North American Hunting Club

Photo Credits

Unless otherwise noted, all black & white photos and illustrations in this book were provided by author Monte Burch. All other works are credited to their source. The cover photo was provided by Daniel J. Cox.

The Author

Monte Burch grew up in the waterfowl rich country of central Missouri near the town of Clinton. In the days of his youth, he hunted mallards in the flooded river and creek bottoms near his home and geese in the grain fields to the north. These days, the area inundated by Truman Reservoir offers even more diverse waterfowl hunting that he still enjoys.

Monte is a full-time freelance writer specializing in outdoor and how-to subjects. He is the author of over 50 books and thousands of magazine and newspaper articles as well as the creator of the "Good Earth Almanac" newspaper strip. Monte writes regularly for most of the outdoor and how-to magazines and is also well know as a photographer and illustrator. He produced most of the photographs and hand-drawn illustrations appearing in the North American Hunting Club's *Modern Waterfowl Hunting*.

In addition to his freelance writing, illustrating and photography, Monte and his wife, Joan, are owners of Outdoor World Press, Inc., publishers of books on a variety of sporting and outdoor topics.

Monte's books have led many hunters and fishermen to great days afield and afloat.

Monte lives and works on an Ozark hill farm near Humansville, Missouri with his wife and three children.

1

Why Hunt Waterfowl?

Why hunt waterfowl? That is indeed a question often asked by hunters hunkered in a tiny blind on a freezing windswept point; by hunters riding an open boat through heavy seas; by hunters chopping ice to remove decoys; and by hunters trying to gather up decoys with frozen fingers.

It's also a question often asked by non-waterfowling friends and relatives—especially spouses.

The reasons are many. Some are practical, others more intrinsic and often not fully understood by either waterfowlers or non-hunters.

Our Waterfowl Hunting Heritage

Waterfowling has given us a rich heritage. One of the reasons many waterfowlers hunt ducks and geese is because they grew up hunting with their dads, granddads, uncles, cousins and friends. Waterfowling, like many other hunting sports, is a tradition that is quite often handed down from generation to generation.

In days gone by, the passing on of the hunting tradition often included not only the knowledge and family waterfowling "secrets", but the actual hunting spots. It's sad to say, that this happens less these days due to changing land uses.

There is indeed a close camaraderie in the challenge of waterfowling that brings generations closer together, quite often making friends of even the most stubborn parents and youngsters. It gives them something special, something all their own to share!

Being There

Another reason many waterfowlers hunt is simply for the "excuse" of being there. A love affair with the marshes, fields and open waters that waterfowl inhabit keeps many waterfowlers coming back again and again. It is something in the smell of mucky soil, something in the prairie sunrise. And the birds themselves are a good part of this attraction.

The beauty and grace of mallards and pintails gliding in, wings locked. The feather snapping flight of bluebills buzzing a blind like miniature jets. The grandeur and heart stopping excitement of watching a hundred or a thousand big Canada geese fly slowly your way. These are the things that are hard to forget, even for the most blase' outdoor enthusiast.

Expensive Meals

Another reason for hunting is the practical aspect of hunting for food. Although harvesting waterfowl for food was a primary concern of generations past, it plays a relatively small part in today's waterfowling. With the small game bags allowed these days, waterfowl make some of the most expensive meats available. Consider the cost of a dog, boat, decoys, licenses, ammunition, guns, leases, gasoline, etc. Even the best of waterfowlers can't shoot enough "meat" to pay for the cost.

This is not to say that waterfowl is not good eating, indeed it has been "food for kings," and can still be some of the best and most elegant of foods. Each bird taken by waterfowl hunters of today and of the future can be looked on as a succulent morsel plucked from the sky. It's something akin to a gourmet paying for a meal in fancy restaurant. Less expensive food would be just as nourishing, but not nearly as special.

It's Like No Other Hunting

The reason many waterfowlers hunt, however, is for the sheer pleasure and the challenge of hunting ducks and geese! It's that simple.

Waterfowling requires special skills in calling, boating, dog training, and shooting; not to mention a naturalist's eye for identifying fast moving birds. These are all skills that require dedication and practice to become adept. Though one or two of these skills are

There is something special about an early-morning marsh that makes just being there a thrill. The diversity of waterfowl species and the conditions under which they are hunted makes waterfowl hunting a very personal sport.

critical to any type of hunting, the pursuit of no other species puts them together the same way waterfowling does!

Though North American waterfowling is firmly rooted in tradition, its practice is quite varied from species to species, flyway to flyway, region to region and family to family. And that is another reason for it's popularity.

Regardless of age, experience, or what part of the country you hunt in, there's something for everyone when it comes to waterfowl hunting. There's black duck shooting on the East Coast, Brant hunting in the West. There's Canada goose hunting in the Midwest, snows and blues in Texas, divers to hunt on the Great Lakes, pintails in the South and mallards almost everywhere!

A Look Ahead

Old-time waterfowlers often lament the past when they recall, "the sky was black with ducks." These days waterfowling does face a rather uncertain future. Populations of waterfowl are dependent on many things, but most importantly weather, nesting conditions and availability of suitable habitat in summer nesting areas, fall migration routes and wintering areas.

Complex as the systems for determining season lengths and bag limits might seem, it's really quite simple. If there is plenty of food along with safe nesting and resting areas there will be plenty of waterfowl. If not, the populations decline.

Because of the variety of needs by the various species, some birds are on the rise, while others are declining—some quite rapidly. This is a continuously changing cycle that will affect different hunters differently in the years ahead, just as it has done in years past.

A good example is the Canada goose. Once down to dangerously low populations, the majestic honker population has increased considerably. This is due to both extensive wildlife management across the country, including raising local flocks, and changing land use. On the other hand, mallards, which are the most popularly gunned waterfowl in the country, have as of late seen serious decline in populations due to bad weather during several consecutive breeding seasons and more importantly, the destruction of nesting habitat.

Wildlife management has never been a static field, and there are opportunities to improve and maintain healthy, populations of most waterfowl species. But it will take all of us, both hunters and non-hunters pulling together to assure the future of both waterfowl and waterfowling.

Hunting waterfowl is one of the most interesting, exciting and challenging of sports. It has had a glorious and colorful history in North America, but if our children are to experience the thrills of waterfowl hunting, then we must all plan for the future.

Learning to successfully hunt the various species of ducks and geese is a lifetime learning process. It provides pleasure and knowledge of the natural world around us for both young and old.

This book is my thanks to all the waterfowlers with whom I have had the good fortune to share a boat or blind. Each and every one has taught me more about the excitement of waterfowling. I hope I can pass the mysteries, excitement and pleasure of the waterfowler's world to others with this book, and do my part in seeing that my children have the opportunity to find their own answer to the question, "Why hunt waterfowl?"

2

Learning To Identify Waterfowl

One of the really fascinating aspects of waterfowling is the variety of species from which hunters have to choose. It can also present one of the biggest problems.

Identification Is Conservation

Because of the varying climatic and habitat requirements of each species, some birds may have high populations while others are experiencing reduced or declining populations. The management answer to this phenomenon is to encourage hunting of the abundant species and limit the kill of the waning species. This is, of course, done by establishing bag limits and season frameworks.

An increasingly popular method for limiting the harvest of less abundant duck species is the *point system* in which different species or the different sexes of the different species have their own point values. This allows for a controlled harvest of birds to avoid removing too many of a species that has a low population, yet allows more liberal limits on species that have high populations.

The point system works like this. Say for example you're hunting ducks in Wisconsin, a state that has used the point system for a number of years. Based on a outline established by the U.S. Fish & Wildlife Service, the state assigns a specific point value to various species and sexes within those species. This is generally done each year to accommodate changes in duck populations.

A populous species like teal may have a value of 10 points while more uncommon ducks like redheads may have a 100-point value. Other species like mallards, wood ducks and pintails would fall somewhere in between with 25-, 35-, 50- or 75-point values.

You reach your daily bag limit when the total point value of the ducks you down reaches or exceeds 100 points. If the first duck you take is a 100-pointer, you are done hunting for the day. But by carefully identifying the ducks before you shoot, you can legally take up to 10 ducks per day.

Under the point system, the law also provides a safeguard for misidentification. If you've already taken three 25-point ducks (75 points worth) then kill a 75-pointer, you're still within the legal limit. The bag limit is reached with the duck that brings your total number of points to 100 or more. Even so, the advantage of larger limits goes to the hunter who can identify the various species and sexes of ducks on the wing. He will be able to extend his hunting enjoyment and take more ducks by concentrating on the low-point species.

Though good waterfowl identification skills can increase the hunter's limit and pleasure under the point system, they're probably even more important for hunters under the traditional bag limit systems. The laws they must abide don't provide a margin for error.

Under this kind of system, an overall bag limit of ducks is established, again following guidelines put forth by the USFWS. Often it reads something like this: "A daily bag limit shall consist of six ducks, of which no more than two may be mallards, no more than three may be wood ducks, and no more than one may be a canvasback *or* redhead."

Though at first glance the traditional system may seem more simple, it really puts the pressure on the hunter. After he takes those two mallards, he has broken the law if he makes an identification error and takes another! The results can be embarrassing and costly!

So, in either situation the first and most important waterfowl hunting skill to learn is identification of the various species in all situations, including in the air, on water or land, and in hand. Each species of waterfowl has it's own unique physical characteristics, habitat preference and habits. By knowing them you'll be well on your way to certain identification of ducks on the wing and in hand. These skills are not difficult to learn, and the learning process itself can be interesting, fun and educational. Besides, practicing identifying ducks can make waterfowling a year round sport!

In learning to identify waterfowl, you'll find you're becoming a better hunter.

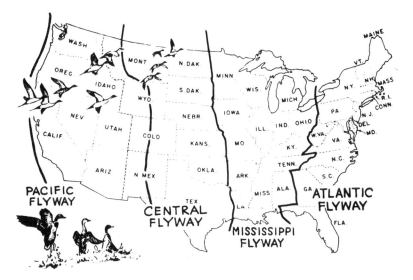

This map outlines the administrative flyways recognized by the U.S. Fish & Wildlife Service. They follow the actual biological flyways as closely as possible.—From drawing by Bob Hines, Bureau of Sport Fisheries & Wildlife.

Flyways

The various species of waterfowl occur in varying numbers over North America. There are certain regions that specific species favor. These regions are divided into four distinct flyways extending from the top of North America down through the United States and into Mexico and South America. The four flyways are: Atlantic, Mississippi, Central and Pacific.

Identifying Waterfowl At A Distance

Waterfowl seen at a distance can be identified by seven basic characteristics. These include: (1) *flock action*, (2) *flight pattern of the individual birds*, (3) *silhouette or shape of the bird*, (4) *color pattern or plumage of the bird*, (5) *landing and taking off pattern*, (6) *vocalizations*, and (7) *habitat*.

When birds are seen at a great distance, the most important identification is the action of the entire flock. Some species don't have as distinguished flock characteristics as others, while some are quite identifiable.

The silhouette or shape of the individual bird is quite often the next important identifying characteristic. As distant birds move closer, you can usually determine the body, head and tail shape of individual birds within a flock. With a little practice, it's quite easy to distinguish various species, though some silhouettes such as those of bluebills and ring-necks will appear quite similar.

As the birds move even closer, the next thing that is usually apparent is the color and plumage pattern of the bird. Brilliantly colored birds such as wood ducks are easy to distinguish. Those less conspicuously hued, such as gadwalls and hens of many species, may be somewhat tougher to correctly identify. For this reason, color is not a particularly consistent identifying characteristic.

Early in the season many drakes will still be in their summer plumage. This is also called the eclipse plumage. It is much less colorful than their mating plumage and quite often looks like that of an adult hen. Teal and shovelers, in particular, are two species known to often migrate before they are out of their ''eclipse'' plumage.

The flight pattern of individual birds is also an identifying feature, even at a distance for some species. Pintails, for instance, fly with outstretched necks. Wood ducks fly with heads cocked up to one side, geese with outstretched necks, etc.

The speed of the wing beats is also a good identifying characteristic as well. This, however, takes a bit more experience to determine. In general, the wing beats of diver ducks are much faster than those of puddle ducks because their wings are smaller in relation to their bodies.

How a bird lands or takes off from water or land also is a good method of identification. Puddle ducks, like mallards and pintails, flush with a sudden burst of wing beats, much like they were on springs. Diver ducks, such as bluebills or canvasbacks, however, must run or patter along the water before they can take off. In landing, puddlers just drop straight down on to the water without much splash. Divers glide in and send water spraying in all directions.

The sounds that the birds make are also important for proper identification. There are ducks that quack, those that whistle, some that grunt and even those that squeal. The sounds their wings make in flight are also important. Each has its own characteristic sound. Knowing these sounds can help identify waterfowl that you can't see.

Although habitat can not be used consistently in identifying waterfowl, it can to some degree be used as a general indication of what kind of ducks you're likely to encounter on a particular trip. For instance, diver ducks won't be seen feeding in cornfields, nor will

Waterfowl identification, both in-hand and on the wing, is a crucial skill to master no matter what type of regulations you're hunting under.

some of the limited range waterfowl such as northern sea ducks be found very far from their open water habitat.

Look for puddle ducks to frequent small ponds, streams or bay areas of large lakes. Divers prefer bigger water and are often seen far from shorelines.

There are four primary groups of waterfowl that are hunted; puddle ducks, divers, sea ducks and geese. There are others that are hunted on a limited basis in localized areas, and we will discuss those fully in a separate chapter.

Puddle ducks feed by tipping up and reaching under the water as far as they can with their usually long necks.

Puddle Ducks

Puddle ducks such as mallards, pintails and numerous others inhabit the fresh water marshes and river systems across the country. They prefer shallow water for feeding and will normally "tip up" or "dabble," reaching under water with their bills to grasp vegetation, their rear ends and feet waving comically in the air. Their legs are located fairly close to the center of their bodies. They are quite sure footed and can walk and run easily on land. Their diet is mostly made up of vegetable matter and they feed readily on crops such as corn, milo, wheat, etc. Because of these feeding traits they generally make the tastiest table fare for the hunter.

Puddle ducks sit higher in the water than divers and when they take off from water or land, they spring straight up. They have smaller feet than diving ducks and the hind toe is not lobed. The colored wing patch, or speculum on most puddle ducks is usually of an iridescent, bright, metallic color. It is one of the most readily distinguishable field identification marks.

Puddle ducks, like the pintail, ride higher on the surface of the water than do diving ducks.

Mallard. Mallards have the dubious distinction of being the most hunted duck in North America. Even back to the days of Nash Buckingham and the tradition known as the "duck club" the mallard has been considered the king of ducks. Even today, you'll find hunters who consider only the mallard and the pintail above "trash

Puddle ducks, like the mallard, spring straight into the air on take-off.

duck'' status. Thankfully, the mallard is generally one of the most numerous species as well.

Mallards are among the largest ducks, weighing about 2 1/2 to 3 pounds. The drake's green shiny head provides the popular nickname ''green head.''

They are found in all flyways and will winter as far north as they can find open water. They fly with a strong, direct flight pattern. Their flock pattern is usually a loose, irregular group. Sometimes they form a distinct ''V'' when traveling over some distance at high altitudes.

These black and white illustrations done by the author are provided to show the light to dark relationship of waterfowl colorations as they may appear to a hunter under low light conditions. A knowledge of these relationships is essential to correct waterfowl identification in the field, because much hunting is done early and late in the day and in poor weather.

Full-color identification illustrations are provided in the Ducks Unlimited Field Guide section of this book. Color is most helpful when identifying the birds when seen on the water, in hand or under bright conditions.

Mallards

   The colors of the drake are easily distinguished with green head, rust chest, white neck ring and white belly. The speculum on the wings of both sexes is bright blue, edged with white on both sides.
   The mallard hen is mottled brown, with white trimmed blue speculums. She has bright orange feet and her underwings are white.
   The hen is more vocal than the drake, making a fairly loud single "quack" in flight. The drake makes a softer, lower pitched sound. In another chapter, we'll discuss in detail other calls of the mallard and how they can help the hunter.

Pintails

Pintail. Pintails, also called ''sprig,'' are also fairly large ducks although usually not as large as mallards. They are found in all flyways but are most common in the western United States and in some parts of the South.

Their long necks and tails are quite easily distinguished in flight, however, the female does not have the long tail feather which gives this species its name.

Pintails are fast flying birds, often making a graceful, spiraling landing from great heights. Just as often, they have a frustrating habit of circling decoys for some time before making up their minds to pitch in.

They have a greenish-brown speculum with a white border on the back. The bill and underwings of both sexes are gray with black on mature birds; almost as if someone had painted these sleek birds with a racing stripe. The breast of the male in breeding plumage is a creamy white, while the female is a light buff color.

Drakes make a sharp whistling sound while the hens make a soft quacking sound.

Black Duck. The black duck is considered the wariest of all wa-

Black Ducks

terfowl. It is found primarily in the Atlantic and Mississippi flyways. It has a sooty, charcoal appearance with a somewhat lighter colored head. Its feet and bill are bright orange to red. The underwing is brilliant white; an identifying mark during flight.

The wing patch is blue to purple without the white border, with the exception of an occasional small patch on the wing tips. This characteristic is very important for telling the difference between a hen mallard and a black duck in hand!

Black ducks fly in small flocks, in V's or waving lines. The call is quite similar to that of the mallard.

Green-Winged Teal. The smallest of North American ducks is the green-winged teal. It seldom weighs more than 12 ounces.

Green-winged teal often stay as far north as open water can be found and nest as far north as Alaska. The green-winged teal is found in all four flyways.

Eclipse colors feature a green patch extending from the eye to the nape of the neck. Teal usually migrate fairly early in the season and are often still in their dull summer plumage. Because both have iridescent green wing patches, they are often mistaken for blue-winged teal. The green-winged, however, lacks the pale blue forewing patch.

Green-winged teal often fly in large flocks, twisting and turning as a unit. Their wing beats are fast and they make a whistling sound.

The males make a low whistle and ''tittering'' sound in flight, while the hens only make a soft quack.

Cinnamon Teal. Unlike other teal, cinnamon teal rarely fly in large groups. They are most often found in pairs or even singly. They are very trusting and not readily alarmed. Cinnamon teal are rarely found east of the Rocky Mountains.

The name cinnamon teal comes from the distinguishing body color of the male, a deep rust color. They have both the fore and aft wing patch which is very similar to the blue-winged teal.

The cinnamon teal's flight pattern is quite similar to that of other teal; twisting, darting and turning. The males sometimes utter a high pitched, soft chatter. The hens, a faint quack.

Blue-Winged Teal. The most common teal, the blue-winged, is the earliest waterfowl to migrate. Although quite small, they're very tasty birds that are found in all flyways. They are distinguished by the bright blue upper wing coverts edged with white. The male has a distinguishable slate blue head with a white crescent behind the bill.

Their flock flight patterns are quite similar to other teal. They usually fly as compact, irregular flocks, maneuvering like tiny fight-

Blue-winged Teal

er jets; twisting, darting, turning all as one unit. They usually fly fairly low which makes their acrobatics seem even more challenging.

The males make an easily discerned whistle while the hens make a soft quack.

Shovelers. The large spoon-shaped bill is easily the most identifiable mark of this bird. There is a blue forewing patch on both sexes and the male has a dark green head. He has a dark brown belly and sides. The hen's body plumage is a dull, mottled brown.

Shovelers are usually early migrators and they fly in a steady, direct flight that makes them ''easy'' targets. Although they are puddle ducks, a good portion of their diet consists of snails and aquatic insects rooted from a marsh or lake bottom with their specialized bill. Often they are not as tasty as other puddle duck species.

They have a green to black speculum and are quite a colorful bird. They usually fly in small irregular flocks. The male makes a soft ''tucka-tucka-tucka'' sound and the hen a soft quack.

Gadwall. Gadwall are also relatively early migrators. Their coloring causes both sexes to be mistaken on the water for female mallards. The most distinguishing feature of the bird is the white speculum with a dark brown to black streak through it.

Shovelers

The gadwall flies in small, compact flocks. They are very fast fliers and usually fly in a direct line. The males make a soft whistling sound and a soft ''kack-kack,'' and the females make a soft quack.

Wigeon. Wigeon have the common name ''baldpate'' because of the white patch on the forehead. These medium sized ducks are fairly nervous and alarm quite easily. They have a white forewing and belly that make a good in-flight identifying mark. The speculum is brown to black. The drake's white to gray head is quite striking with its green eye patch.

Wigeons fly in small flocks with quick, erratic flight. Their wings make a soft, rustling sound in flight. They often settle in with divers and rob them of food. They are sometimes locally known as ''robber ducks.''

Gadwalls

Widgeon

The drakes make a soft whistling sound and the females a loud, drawn out "kack."

Wood Duck. There is no argument that the wood duck is probably the most beautiful and colorful duck in North America. The brilliantly colored iridescent plumage on its chest is flecked with white and the distinctive iridescent bluegreen head is streaked with white.

Although the medium sized duck is found in all four North American flyways, it is most common in the Atlantic and Mississippi. It is most often found around small streams, ponds and lakes with thick timber.

Wood ducks fly fast with a direct manner and are usually found in small flocks. They have a distinct flight pattern, often twisting their heads from side to side. Their bill is usually pointed down, giving the head a sort of "cocked" appearance while they fly. Wood ducks have a blue or purple wing patch without heavy borders of white.

The males make a soft "hooooooing" sound in flight while the females make a loud "criiiiack" sound when startled.

Wood Duck

Diving ducks, like the canvasback, must run along the water to take flight.

Diving Ducks

The habitat of diving ducks is usually the open waters of coastal bays, larger lakes and rivers. These days, they may also inhabit the larger, man-made reservoirs, often providing hunters with the opportunity to take both diver and puddle ducks from the same blind.

These ducks are called divers because they feed by diving. They can and often do dive very deep. Their diet consists mostly of aquatic plants with mollusks, shellfish and fish taking a distant second.

The meat of some diver species may have a bit stronger flavor than that of puddle ducks, but such is not always the case. Canvasbacks, for example, have a diet which consists almost exclusively of eel grass and wild celery. This diet makes their meat among the most succulent and best eating of all waterfowl.

The bodies of diver ducks are shaped somewhat differently than puddle ducks. Their legs are set well back from the body's midpoint, making them awkward on land, but great swimmers. They have large feet with a lobed hind toe and will often dive and swim underwater for great distances to escape danger.

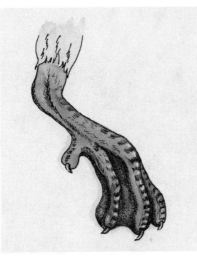

The feet of diving duck species are quite large and the hind toes are lobed.

Because their wings are smaller in relation to their bodies, they must patter or run across the surface of the water to take off. Their wing beats are much faster than those of puddle ducks to make up for the reduced wing surface. They also have shorter tails and sit lower in the water. Because of the short tails, they usually use their feet as rudders while in flight and you can often see their feet waving wildly as they fly or try to land.

The color of their speculum is usually duller and not iridescent.

Bufflehead. Buffleheads are small diving ducks and among the tiniest of all ducks. They are usually found in small flocks flying very low over the water. They are fairly late migrators and through the winter will be found as far North as there is open water.

The conspicuous black and white pattern of the drake identifies them quite readily as does their large "puffy" shaped head.

Buffleheads are normally silent, but occasionally they will utter a faint squeak or weak quack. Their wing patch is white.

Golden Eye. Also called "whistlers or whistler ducks" because of the distinct whistling sound their wings make in flight, these fairly large divers nest in tree cavities. They are most often found on deep bodies of water with lots of surrounding timber and on fast flowing rivers which are among the last waters to freeze up in the North Country. They are found on both coasts and throughout the Central and Mississippi flyways as well.

Golden eyes are identified in flight by their distinctive black and white markings. When taking off from the water they rise in a fast spiral. The wing patch is white. The males make a high-pitched pier-

Buffleheads

Golden Eyes

cing call, while the hens make a low quack.

Golden eyes are fast ducks and expert fliers. They are very difficult to kill and the conditions under which they are most available to the hunter are often the worst imaginable. All of this adds up to make the make them a very sporting species to hunt, if not the best table fare.

Canvasback. Weighing up to three pounds, the canvasback is one of the largest ducks. A strong and fast flier, canvasbacks fly in irregular V's and lines. They are fairly late migrators and fly with loud sounding wing beats.

Canvasbacks have a distinguishable sloping forehead. The wing speculum on ''cans'' is gray, uniformly colored like the rest of the wing. The drakes have a rust colored head, a dark breast and white belly. They somewhat resemble redheads except for the can's greater size and the shape of its head.

The drakes make a loud croaking and growling sound while the females produce a quack much like that of a mallard.

Canvasbacks

Redheads

Redhead. The redhead resembles the canvasback in appearance, but is somewhat smaller. The shape of the head is also more rounded and its color tends more toward gray than brown. These beautiful birds are found coast to coast, often intermingled with flocks of canvasbacks.

Redheads migrate in large flocks, usually flying in V's or lines. Flight pattern is fast and direct. The wing patch is light gray and fairly indistinguishable from the rest of the wing.

The males make a purring growl while the hens make a loud, high-pitched quack.

Scaup. Also called "bluebills" or "broadbills," there are both lesser and greater varieties of scaup. Both are quite similar in appearance, and most hunters, short of waterfowl biologists, can not tell them apart.

One of the latest migrants, scaup usually travel just ahead of the freeze up.

Scaup

The males are dark on both ends and white in the middle while the females are a fairly even brown. Both sexes have blue bills, hence the name. A good identifying field mark is a light strip on the wing. This strip is half a wing length on lesser scaup and almost two thirds on the greater scaup.

Scaup fly in tight compact bunches, twisting and darting, and are usually found only on large bodies of water. They are very restless while on the water. They are continually moving about, flying for short distances then landing again. On the water, they form large groups known as "rafts."

Their wings make a buzzing sound and the drakes make a "BRRRRRRR"-type growling sound while the hens are usually silent. Wing patch is white.

Ring-Necked Duck. Quite similar in both appearance and habit to scaup, ring-necks are often found in the same flocks with scaup. The major difference for field identification are the white rings around the bill which scaup don't have. They also have a light brown ring around the neck, however, this is not very visible. The wing patch is a light gray.

Ring-necks usually fly in fairly open formation and will often come straight into decoys without any circling or hesitation. More than most diving ducks, ring-necks can be found on small-water-type habitat; especially on river systems and large inland marshes.

The males make a soft purring sound, hens are silent.

Ruddy Duck. One of the smallest of ducks, this trusting little duck usually swims away or dives rather than flying. The male is a deep rusty brown with a black head, white cheek patch and a blue bill. The hen is gray and has a cheek patch divided by a brown bar.

While on the water the fan-like tail on both sexes stands stiffly erect and makes an easy identifying mark. These little ducks have a

Ruddy Ducks

hard time getting off the water and fly with a noisy wing beat and halting pace. They are found on both coasts and occasionally on the Great Lakes.

The wing patch is gray. Both sexes are usually silent.

Common Merganser. One of the largest ducks, the merganser is also among the latest to migrate. It has a black back with pink chest and sides.

The Common Merganser has a conspicuous white belly which shows more white in flight than other species. The drake has a green head and red bill.

The merganser's flight is extremely strong and swift and usually low over the water in a "follow-the-leader" fashion.

The wing patch is white. The only sound is an occasional croak.

Common Mergansers

Red-Breasted Merganser. A bit smaller than the common merganser, the flight characteristics are similar. There is, however, less white shown in flight. The drake has an orange chest speckled with black. Wing patches are white streaked with black.

The red-breasted merganser is found primarily along both coasts as well as in the Gulf of Mexico.

Seldom heard by hunters, red-breasted mergansers croak only occasionally.

Hooded Merganser. Found in inland waters of all the coastal states, the hooded is the smallest of all the mergansers. The characteristic markings include two prominent black bars between the chest and sides. The drake has an readily identifiable white hood. It has yellow eyes and the bill is black, and toothed, as are the fish catching bills of all mergansers.

They are usually found only in small flocks or pairs. Hooded mergansers are extremely strong fliers and their wings often move so fast they appear as a blur.

Wing patches on the hooded merganser are gray with black. These ducks make an occasional croak.

Many hunters call mergansers "fish ducks." They don't have a reputation of being great table fare.

Geese

Probably the most distinguishing characteristic of geese is that they are usually much bigger than ducks. There are, however, some geese that are not much bigger than a big, red-leg mallard. Their

Canada Goose

wing beats are usually much slower and they usually fly in a V or long, wavering line. They will fly in loose flocks when moving around local areas. As a rule, they also fly at higher altitudes than ducks.

The in-flight silhouette of the geese is also important. Their necks are longer and more stretched out and they have large, fan-shaped, easily seen tails.

All species of geese have their legs situated fairly close to the center of their bodies, enabling them to walk on land quite easily. Like puddle ducks, they spring up into the air when flushed. Geese are amazingly fast and agile for their size.

Canada Goose. There are a number of different varieties of Canada goose in North America, however, their markings are quite similar. There are actually 11 known subspecies. About the only difference is their size. The largest may weigh as much as 16 pounds or more; the smallest about four to five pounds. They are easily recognized with their long black neck and head, white chin strap and black bill. The remainder of their body consists of varied shades of gray brown. The belly near the tail is white.

Geese make a number of loud vocalizations. The most common one is a loud "kerhonking" that can be a single note or several strung together. This sound is the source of the common name "honker."

Snow Goose. The snow goose is not as large as the Canada, and the adults are all white except for black wing tips. Yearling geese are dirty gray or brown. There is also a dark phase of the snow goose called a blue goose. The blue goose has a bluish gray body with a white head and neck. Previously, some hunters and biologists thought that snow geese and blue geese were separate species. However, it has been shown that the two color phases interbreed freely with viable offspring. In fact, some studies show that the blue color phase is actually becoming more dominant the the pure white phase.

Because of the habit of flying in long waving lines, the goose is also often called "wavey" particularly by the Indians who hunt the birds on the northern end of their migration routes.

Snow and blues usually travel in large flocks and make a kerhonking sound, though it is much higher pitched and shorter than that of the Canada goose.

White-Fronted Goose. The name for the goose comes from a white band just behind the bill. They are also called "speckle-bellies," because they are a gray color with mottled white and gray undersides.

Blue Goose

Snow Goose

Specklebelly Goose

They travel in large flocks usually in a V formation. They give a high pitched cackling call that has also given them the nickname the "laughing goose." It is among the most difficult of waterfowl calls to imitate.

To goose connoisseurs, the "speck" is considered the most delicious of goose species on the table.

Ross' Goose. Quite similar in appearance to snow geese, these fairly rare geese are quite a bit smaller. Because of their dangerously low populations Ross' geese are not hunted. This makes proper identification of this bird especially important for hunters in areas known to harbor Ross' geese.

In-Hand Identification

Although proper identification of waterfowl is not always possible in the air, it is a definite must in the blind. There are several charts, such as the one shown, that provide a systematic method of determining the species of waterfowl. A good book to take along hunting is the *Key to North American Waterfowl*. The book is printed on plastic, so it should be right at home in a duck blind.

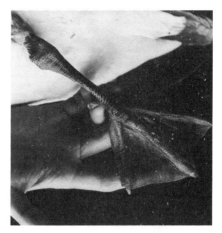

*Size, color and physical characteristics
of a duck or goose's foot can be a good
initial indicator for in-hand identification.*

On the following two pages is a chart produced by and provided courtesy of the U.S. Fish & Wildlife Service and the Missouri Department of Conservation. It is a valuable aid in recognizing duck species in-hand, after they've been bagged.

Simply start at the top of the page and answer the first question. Then follow the black lines to secondary choices until proper identification is made.

Both the USFWS and the Missouri Department of Conservation encourage hunters to learn the birds' silhouettes, flight mannerisms, wing beat, speeds of flight and color patterns on bodies and wings. When every effort is made to recognize a duck before it is shot, hunters are able to take the greatest advantage of their sport and enjoy their time afield to the fullest.

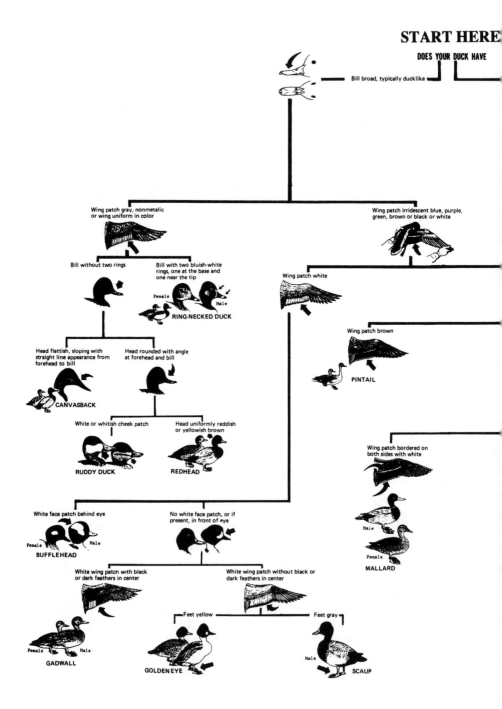

START HERE

DOES YOUR DUCK HAVE

Bill broad, typically ducklike

Wing patch gray, nonmetalic or wing uniform in color

Wing patch irridescent blue, purple, green, brown or black or white

Bill without two rings

Bill with two bluish-white rings, one at the base and one near the tip

Female   Male
RING-NECKED DUCK

Wing patch white

Wing patch brown

PINTAIL

Head flattish, sloping with straight line appearance from forehead to bill

Head rounded with angle at forehead and bill

CANVASBACK

White or whitish cheek patch

Head uniformly reddish or yellowish brown

RUDDY DUCK   **REDHEAD**

Wing patch bordered on both sides with white

Male

Female
MALLARD

White face patch behind eye

No white face patch, or if present, in front of eye

Female   Male
BUFFLEHEAD

White wing patch with black or dark feathers in center

White wing patch without black or dark feathers in center

Feet yellow

Feet gray

Female   Male
GADWALL

GOLDENEYE

Male
SCAUP

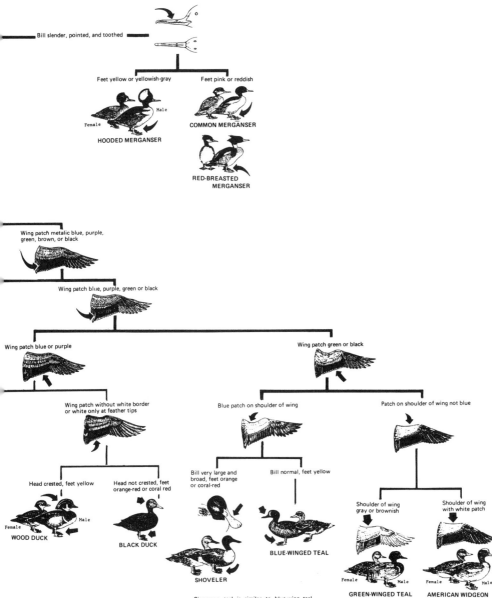

Bill slender, pointed, and toothed

Feet yellow or yellowish-gray

Feet pink or reddish

Male

Female

COMMON MERGANSER

HOODED MERGANSER

RED-BREASTED
MERGANSER

Wing patch metallic blue, purple,
green, brown, or black

Wing patch blue, purple, green or black

Wing patch blue or purple

Wing patch green or black

Wing patch without white border
or white only at feather tips

Blue patch on shoulder of wing

Patch on shoulder of wing not blue

Head crested, feet yellow

Head not crested, feet
orange-red or coral red

Bill very large and
broad, feet orange
or coral-red

Bill normal, feet yellow

Shoulder of wing
gray or brownish

Shoulder of wing
with white patch

Female

Male

WOOD DUCK

BLACK DUCK

BLUE-WINGED TEAL

SHOVELER

Female

Male

Female

Male

GREEN-WINGED TEAL

AMERICAN WIDGEON

Cinnamon teal is similar to blue-wing teal
except that male cinnamon teal is reddish on
head and underparts. The female is virtually
identical to the female blue-wing teal.

Female American widgeon has brown breast and
flank. Female green-wing teal has gray speckled
breast and flank.

Preferred Waterfowl Plant Foods

Knowing the various feeding habits and the preferred foods of waterfowl not only helps in identifying birds in the wild, but will also help determine the best feeding spots. The chart illustrates the favorite foods of many waterfowl.

Acorns—One of the favorite foods of most puddle ducks, especially mallards, pintails, wood ducks and black ducks.

Aneilema—Also a good food for mallards, black and pintails.

Barnyard Grass—Grows well in wet soil and is a favored food of many puddle ducks.

Buckwheat—One of the cultivated foods that is a favorite of puddle ducks.

Bulrush—A very important duck food in the Gulf states.

Chufa—A favorite of both mallards and pintails.

Corn—One of the most preferred foods of all puddle ducks, especially mallards. Also the preferred food of geese.

Delta Arrowhead—A lower Mississippi Gulf Coast food loved by mallards, ring-necked ducks, pintails and canvasbacks.

Eel Grass—One of the favorite foods of divers. Eel grass thrives only in waters with a current.

Flatsedge—A favorite of puddle ducks in the coastal gulf states.

Millet—There are several varieties, both wild and cultivated, that are favorites of puddle ducks.

Smartweed—A favorite of many puddle ducks.

Wigeongrass—Requires brackish water, but is a favorite with both divers and puddle ducks.

Rice—Both wild and domestic rice are favored duck foods where ever they are available.

Winter Wheat—A favorite of geese.

Ducks Unlimited
Wing Watcher's Guide

(During their 50th Anniversary Ducks Unlimited has generously agreed to supply this color identification section for the North American Hunting Club's *Modern Waterfowl Hunting*.)

Picture a flock of bluebills suspended over choppy water, battling a stiff headwind. Imagine snow geese blanketing a field in white. Watch the wary black duck as he circles, looks and circles one more time. Waterfowl all. Hardy, yet fragile, they pour out of the north country, signaling the coming of winter. And they trickle back toward the end of the cold months, spring sunshine trailing behind.

There was a time, they say, when their numbers would blacken the sky. Nesting on wetlands created 10,000 years ago by glaciers of the last ice age, waterfowl numbering upwards of 400 million followed their annual migratory routes at the turn of this century. Disease, drought, floods and other whims of nature were their primary enemies.

That is, until man started to encroach upon the breeding grounds. "Drain the swamp," the developers cried. And they did. Ten acres here, 50 there, 100 more down the line.

And so it went for years. Some did it to make a living and to simply carve out a place to call their own. Others were bent on a fast buck. United States wetland acreage, which has been estimated at 216 million acres in the late 1700s, has dropped to less than 92 million. An additional 458,000 acres, an area the size of Rhode Island, is lost each year.

During the 1930s, problems created by the loss of wetlands were further compounded by a scorching drought. The heat of the sun and high winds transformed mid-America and the Canadian prairies into a "Dust Bowl" nightmare, and North America's wild waterfowl numbers dwindled to less than 30 million birds. But a group of far-sighted sportsmen calling themselves the "More Game Birds in American Foundation" was not content to accept the loss sitting down. Members of the unique outfit initiated an extensive aerial survey of North American waterfowl and determined that some 70 percent of these ducks and geese used Canada's prairie pothole region for critical nesting sites.

It was clear that money was needed to preserve and restore the disappearing Canadian wetlands before it was too late. Something had to be done, and it was impossible to turn to the federal government for help. By law, funds from United States Migratory Waterfowl Stamps and the newly-enacted Federal Aid in Wildlife Restoration Act (Pittman-Robertson) could not be expended in a foreign country.

In 1937 Ducks Unlimited became the first international waterfowl conservation organization. Its aim was to do what no one else could—preserve and restore the essential wetlands of North America. More Game Birds in America transferred all of its assets to the newly-formed Ducks Unlimited organization, and a fight to save wetlands habitat began, the likes of which the conservation world had never seen before. Since then, DU has raised nearly $400 million, with nearly 80 cents from each dollar earmarked for habitat. Some 3,300 wetland conservation projects have been completed. Over four million acres of habitat are under reservation, including in excess of 16,000 protective shoreline miles.

If you've ever seen a flock of mallards cock their wings and swing wide for a final approach. If you've ever seen a wood duck dodge and dart its way through a stand of flooded timber...you are not alone in your appreciation of some of nature's spectacles.

Some very special people marveled at these same sights and sounds 50 years ago. They were the ones who decided that something must be done to preserve the magic. Ducks Unlimited is continuing a program designed to do just that.

About The Artist

Angus H. Shortt produced these original paintings for *Sports Afield* magazine. They appeared monthly for three years beginning in January 1946, and were published in book form in 1948 titled *Know Your Ducks And Geese*.

Shortt joined Ducks Unlimited in 1939 as an artist-technician. He became the art director in 1965, and in addition to routine duties, Shortt prepared the maps and graphics and was otherwise deeply involved in the production of many waterfowl movies Ducks Unlimited Canada produced between 1940-55.

Shortt, now 80, retired from DU in 1973. He continues to work and support the organization by donations of his art.

Mallards

Pintails

**Black
Ducks**

**Green-winged
Teal**

**Blue-winged
Teal**

**Cinnamon
Teal**

Shovelers

Wood Ducks

Wigeon

Gadwalls

Canvasbacks

**Common
  Golden Eye**

Redhead

Lesser
Scaup

Greater
Scaup

**Ring-necked
Ducks**

Buffleheads

Ruddy Duck

Surf
Scoter

Black
Scoter

White-winged
Scoter

Harlequin Ducks

Old Squaw

Canada Geese

Snow Geese

White-fronted Geese

3

Waterfowl Wing Shooting

The fundamentals of swinging and shooting a shotgun are fairly easy to learn. Almost anyone can master them with a bit of practice.

Rather than aiming at a target as with a rifle or handgun, you simply "point" and shoot. For you to be a consistently good shot, your gun must come up to the same position each time you shoot.

In a perfect situation you should be standing in a balanced stance with your feet spread like a boxer. You bring the gun up, place the stock against your cheek, then against your shoulder. Keeping both eyes open and focused on the moving target, you point the gun at the target and gently "slap" the trigger with your finger.

There are, however, rarely any "ideal" situations when hunting waterfowl. You're either cramped into a tiny wooden blind, lying flat on your back in a small boat covered with camouflage cloth or lying in the cold, frozen mud of a goose feeding field. All make for the least convenient and effective shooting conditions.

Practice, Practice, Practice

The beginning waterfowl hunter must first practice, practice and then practice some more under normal shooting conditions to learn the basics as well as the characteristics of his or her gun. This, however, is not a particularly difficult project, and can be a lot of fun, regardless of whether you do it at a formal shooting club, trap range,

One of the best practice drills for the wing shooter is to point a shotgun into a mirror. Any flaws in style or technique will be quickly apparent.

skeet field or simply gather with a friend or two for some hand-thrown clay pigeon shooting.

Actually using a hand trap or just throwing the targets by hand is the easiest way to simulate most of the shots you will be getting from duck blinds and goose pits. By positioning the thrower and the shooters in different arrangements, you can cover about every angle. *In every case just make sure you have a safe shooting backstop and that the target thrower is well protected.*

As you progress, you may want to look for a shooting club in your area that has a duck tower range. In this shotgunning game, clay targets are thrown from an oscillating trap in a high tower. Nothing else simulates as well the shots a waterfowler, particularly a pass shooter, is likely to encounter in the field.

Methods For Wing Shooting Waterfowl

Once you learn the basics of shotgunning on clay pigeons, you can learn the methods of wing shooting, or taking of birds on the wing. Basically there are three different techniques to wing shooting: 1)*snap shooting, 2)swing-through leading, and 3)sustained lead shooting.*

Some shooters use only one method, others combine methods, and many, like myself, use different methods to suit the various hunting situations.

For close-in shooting, I prefer the fast snap shooting technique. However, when pass shooting high-flying geese, I prefer a sustained lead type of shooting. Basically, here's how each is accomplished.

Snap Shooting. Although this method is primarily used by most hunters on faster upland game such as quail, and rarely on waterfowl, there are times when it can be the most effective. Snap shooting is actually split-second reflex shooting. The shooter spots the target, anticipates where the target will be, mounts his gun and shoots at the spot where he hopes the target and shot will meet.

Swing-Through Lead. This is the most frequently used wing shooting system for waterfowl and also the easiest for beginners to learn. The process is to pick up the target, track it with the gun barrel, increasing the speed of your swing until the gun muzzle swings just past or in front of the bird. Then fire! *Continue your swing-through much in the same manner as for golf or bowling. This follow through is very important as it ensures you won't shoot behind your target.* The amount, or speed of swing-through, is determined by the distance or lead you give the bird. This is very effective for close-in pass shooting.

With both the swing-through and the sustained-lead methods, you must establish a lead on your target and keep the gun moving. Follow-through is the most important key to success.

Sustained Lead Shooting. This technique is the hardest to learn, but the most effective one for pass shooting high-flying birds. In this method you pick a predetermined spot ahead of the moving bird and swing with it, not the bird. *Again remember to continue your swing after the shot to prevent you from shooting behind your target.*

Sounds simple enough, but, you must determine the correct amount of lead necessary by estimating the speed, range and angle at which the bird is flying. That takes some time and experience in the field to accomplish with any rate of consistency. More than one goose hunter has shot at the lead goose in a flock only to hit the second or third one back!

How To Pick The Best Shot

There is a lot more to successful waterfowl wing shooting than just mastering the mechanics of these techniques. Placing your shot properly for a quick clean kill often relies as much on knowledge of specie habits as it does on good shooting skills.

As with most other hunting situations, you can provide yourself an edge if you also know when to shoot as well as how to shoot. For instance, decoying ducks will usually hesitate just moments before settling into decoys, although some species such as teal or woodies may simply drop into your spread like a thrown football. In most instances, waiting until the birds just start to settle provides the oppor-

Don't shoot a shotgun like a rifle. This youngster will have difficulty because he is intently aiming his gun. He is also using the edge of the blind as a rest which will restrict his swing.

Point a shotgun! Don't aim it!

tune time for the best shots. At that point the birds sort of shift into neutral and it takes them extra effort to start climbing back toward the sky.

One of the most difficult shots for most hunters is the straight-in shot. In most instances, unless the bird is definitely creating a pass shooting situation, you will do better to wait until it makes a swing around the decoys.

This brings up a very important aspect of waterfowling which will be covered in detail in another chapter—decoys. Properly set, they can usually set the distance at which most of your shots at decoying birds will be, and of all the problems involved in waterfowl wing shooting, the biggest seems to be judging the range or distance of birds.

An experiment devised to test the effectiveness of steel shot some years back utilized an observer in a duck blind along with a hunter. The hunter would pick his shots, then estimate the range or yardage while the observer used a rangefinding device at the same time. A majority of the hunters misjudged the distance, almost always guessing the birds to be closer in than they actually were!

Regardless of how good a shot you are, shooting beyond the effective clean killing range of your gun and shotshells should not be attempted. If you've ever sat through a day in a crowded public hunting area with skybusting idiots surrounding you, you'll fully appreciate the serious waterfowler who learns to judge distance properly and doesn't shoot at birds that are out of range.

One method you can use to help judge distance of decoying ducks is to place your farthest, or a "marker" decoy, 35 yards from your blind. Then accounting for the angle of birds in flight, you should have shots at nothing more than 45 yards once the birds come in past your marker decoy.

Avoiding Cripples

Pick out a single bird and keep shooting until you drop that bird. More than one cripple has been lost to greedy hunters who tried to take more than one bird from a flight. Only if you're sure you have a clean kill should you attempt to take another bird from a flock.

Nothing will increase your shooting percentage on waterfowl like knowing when the birds are in range and when they are not.

When going for a double, take a distant bird first and save the closest one for the second shot.

Crippled waterfowl can be extremely hard to retrieve, even with good dogs. They hide in brush or dive underwater and hold themselves to underwater vegetation until they drown.

Always take a loaded gun when chasing cripples. Many gunners like to use a load of sixes at this time because the extra number of shot can be a help in hitting a crippled duck sitting in the water. Aim for the head only because a crippled duck will have most of its vital areas submerged.

Making A Double

Experienced gunners won't pick out the easiest or closest bird first. They take the second or third bird back, then if they succeed, they have the nearer bird as their next target. If you pick the closest bird first, by the time you get a chance for another, all of them may be out of range again.

Waterfowling Gun Safety

Of course, all gun safety rules apply, but there are also some special rules that apply for waterfowling. When you are hunting from a boat, place your unloaded gun in the bow of the boat pointing forward before stepping into the boat. The second hunter then steps into the boat and takes the second unloaded gun and places it in the stern pointing backwards. Then the second hunter can shove the boat off and take his position in the stern. Make sure the boat is anchored securely before shooting and that both hunters are in the center of the boat with their firearms pointed away from each other.

If hunting from a canoe, only the front or bow hunter should carry a loaded gun while the stern or rear paddler operates the canoe. Alternate every so often so each hunter has an opportunity to shoot.

When hunting from a blind, lay your unloaded gun on the ground in front of the blind. Then climb into the blind and bring your unloaded gun into it with you. Make sure the muzzle hasn't been clogged with dirt, snow or debris, before loading it with the muzzle pointed in a safe direction. Always hold your gun with the muzzle pointing safely out of the blind, or keep it in holders provided in some blinds. Always unload the gun before leaving the blind and lay it on the outside of the blind before you step out.

Camouflaging Your Gun

Here's where the fun and controversy comes in again. Granted, if you own a premier grade Beretta over/under or Winchester Model 21, you probably don't want to start painting it with a can of duck

When dealing with wary, heavily-hunted waterfowl, it's important to make sure that your gun is well camouflaged.

boat paint, but one of the biggest problems waterfowlers face is shiny guns.

Bill Harper, an expert waterfowler, has the right attitude toward waterfowling guns. He buys the cheapest model of the best gun that suits him, in his case a Beretta, takes it out of the box and paints it completely. This probably won't make me popular with gun manufacturers, but it does make a lot of sense. Shiny stocks and bluing reflect sunlight and can spook ducks and geese. Just make sure you don't lay one of your camouflaged guns down while quail hunting. They are also hard for humans to see. I still haven't found one of mine.

To paint your gun, clean both the wood and metal with a cleaner/degreaser. Then paint it with duck boat paint. You can add camouflage patterns if you like, but the main idea is to provide a dulling look. If you don't want to paint your gun yourself you can buy one of the camouflaged guns now being sold by most of the top manufacturers.

There is, of course, a much simpler method for those who aren't quite "that" serious and also wish to use their gun for upland game or at a respectable gun club. There are a number of gun socks and tape products that can be used to cover your gun and provide both camouflage and protection to the finish.

Gun Care

Waterfowling guns get the most abuse and quite often the least amount of care. They have to endure rain, sleet, freezing weather, mud, ice and sometimes even salt water. However, if properly cared for, they can still provide a lifetime of great waterfowl shooting.

It doesn't matter if the gun is brand new or a valued hand-me-down, a little bit of care can go a long way. The first step starts with a preseason check-up to insure the gun is in proper working order. Then wipe down the exterior with a good rust preventive gun oil, including the stock. If the gun has recently been cleaned, just spray the interior with a rust preventive spray such as WD-40.

If the gun hasn't been cleaned recently, the best bet, particularly for autoloaders that may malfunction due to overloading of grease, is to disassemble the gun as far as you can do easily and wipe everything clean. If this is a bit complicated, and with some models it is, merely use a spray cleaner/degreaser to clean the interior. Squirt the liquid inside the mechanism and stand the gun on end to allow all loosened debris, grease, etc., to flow out. Then wipe clean and *lightly* spray with WD-40. Wipe away all excess oil. Leave standing,

Simple gun care measures will ensure that a firearm keeps functioning reliably and stays looking good, too.

muzzle down for several days to insure that all dirt and debris, as well as excess oil, runs out.

In the field care is even more important. I keep a plastic bag with an oiled rag as well as a couple of clean rags and some WD-40 in my vehicle. At the end of the day when everything else is packed away, I stop and spray the entire gun inside and out with WD-40, then wipe down with a clean rag and finally wipe down with the gun oil soaked rag.

Even with this care, however, you won't be able to get all the moisture from the gun and if you immediately stick a waterfowling gun into a tight gun case, you're going to get into problems. Make sure to reclean the gun again when you get home and, if possible, leave it exposed to the air for a day or so before storing it.

4

Waterfowling Guns
And Loads

Waterfowling guns have literally been everything from huge cannons mounted on punt boats during the old market hunting days to the dainty little .410s better suited to quail coverts.

According to the gun manufacturers, however, the most popular waterfowling gun is a 12 gauge. Recently, there has also been a revival of interest in specialty waterfowl guns. Now almost all manufacturers offer some sort of waterfowling shotgun specially designed just for that purpose. They range from the venerable Marlin 10 gauge, bolt action goose gun to the Remington Special Purpose Magnums.

Today's waterfowlers have a wide variety of guns to choose from, including not only the special waterfowling guns, but those that can also be used for upland game, trap or competitive shooting. With the variety of guns available, as well as interchangeable barrels and/or interchangeable chokes, you can quite easily suit the gun to the specific situation whether it is shooting teal from potholes or pass shooting wary geese on traditional refuge flight paths.

Regardless of which type of gun you prefer, be it a shiny new automatic or a trusty old double, the best gun for you is one with which you can consistently hit and kill waterfowl!

Types Of Waterfowling Guns
There are basically five different types of shotguns: pump, semi-

automatic, bolt action, double barrel and single barrel. Each has its advantages and disadvantages, and most hunters find they shoot better with one type or another. The best method of determining which is best for you is to shoot each type until you find the one that suits you. A description of the advantages and disadvantages of each may help you in your search.

Pump Action Shotguns. Without a doubt, the pump, or the slide action repeater as it is more properly called, is the king of waterfowling shotguns.

There are many advantages of using the pump. Pump guns are fairly lightweight, fast, economical and they carry three shells. (Both the pump and the automatic shotgun are capable of holding more than three shells, but all guns used for hunting migratory game birds in the U.S., must be plugged so they can hold only three shells or less.) Plus, pumps are easy to operate, rarely foul-up or cause problems in cold, wet weather and their long sighting plane helps on longer shots.

Although pumps are not as fast to operate as a double barrel or semi-automatic, I've seen experienced pump shooters get off their second and third shots as fast as many shooters with semi-automatics. Short-action pumps are extremely fast in handling. The relatively short barrels on many of these guns also make them easy to handle in a blind or boat. They are among the best waterfowling guns on the market to start with for the younger or beginning hunter.

Pumps do, however, have a bit more recoil than semi-automatics, mostly due to their lighter weight and their action. Pumps lack the recoil-reducing gas ports of today's automatics. Another disadvantage to the pump is that you can't tell if the gun is loaded or not without working the action. This is a minor disadvantage to most waterfowlers.

Semi-Automatic Shotguns. The second most popular waterfowling guns are the semi-automatics or autoloaders. There are a large number of different models of autoloaders made by the various manufacturers.

Probably the single biggest advantage of these guns is the speed with which they allow hunters to get off their second or third shots. You can snap three shots off just as fast as you can pull the trigger with a semi-auto. Another distinct advantage, particularly when using heavy loads such as for geese, is that semi-automatics have less recoil than all other types of shotguns. Being heavier than other guns, some of the recoil is dampened by the weight of the gun. However, most of it is reduced by the action of the gun itself.

Most any action of shotgun in 10 gauge to 20 gauge can find happiness in the hands of a waterfowler. Each offers distinct advantages and disadvantages.

One of the most famous semi-automatics of all, the Browning, uses a style of recoil dampening called "blowback," which uses the recoil action to operate the mechanism of the gun. This action cuts down on the recoil tremendously.

A good example of this type of action is the Browning Auto-5 Invector Magnum 12 gauge which is chambered for 3-inch shells and has a 30-inch barrel. Weighing 8 pounds 13 ounces, it is a heavy gun but extremely effective in the goose blind or when banging away at wary, big-water bluebills. It comes with an Invector Choke which enables you to change chokes quite easily and a rubber recoil pad is standard issue on the 3-inch Magnum models.

The second method of recoil dampening with a semi-auto shotgun utilizes the gases from the spent shell to operate the mechanism. A good example of this type is the Remington Model 11-87 which is also an extremely popular autoloader. The 12 gauge Magnum models come with 32-, 30- or 28-inch, full choke barrels, or a 28- inch modified. The gun can be used with steel shot without any effect on appearance or performance. Fitted with Remchoke, this popular gun can be used for anything from teal to geese, rabbits to deer. It's an ideal one-gun choice.

Regardless of the methods used, the lessening of recoil allows most shooters to shoot a more consistent series of shots. Without having to readjust after heavy recoil each time, you can keep the gun mounted and speed up the number of shots in a given amount of time. This can make a big difference when you're trying to nail a big old Canada honker on a cold December morning. It's a real cripple saver.

Other good semi-automatics are available from Beretta, Mossberg and Franchi.

One problem with semi-automatics, especially if they aren't kept extremely clean and properly lubricated, is they can hang up in cold weather. Keeping them absolutely clean and free of grease build-up will prevent most of these problems. Another disadvantage to automatics is the flying shells inside a duck blind. More than once I've been pounded against the head by flying empty hulls, only to lose concentration on the bird I was tracking.

In some cases, especially for inexperienced hunters, the ease of taking follow-up shots with a semi-auto can become a disadvantage. Some hunters develop a tendency to use two or even three shots without thinking, when one carefully placed load would have done the trick.

Bolt Action. One type of gun that is well known to serious goose hunters is the Marlin Goose gun. These economical and efficient guns have been bringing down high flying geese for years. The gun is available in the 12 gauge Original Marlin Goose Gun or the newer Marlin Supergoose 10. The 12 gauge comes with 36-inch full choke barrel and 3-inch Magnum capability. It will easily handle either lead or steel shot and has a 2-shot clip magazine. They come with a ventilated recoil pad and leather carrying strap. The 10 gauge model has a 34-inch full choke barrel, weighs 10 1/2 pounds and also comes with a sling and rubber recoil pad. The latter is a monster usually selected by goose specialists. It does the job when almost everything else fails.

The long barrels of these guns provide both advantages and disadvantages. The long sighting plane is good for locking on high- flying geese. The length, however, make the guns somewhat awkward to handle in the confines of a blind. The bolt handle action is probably the slowest type of gun to fire, although the heavy-duty firepow-

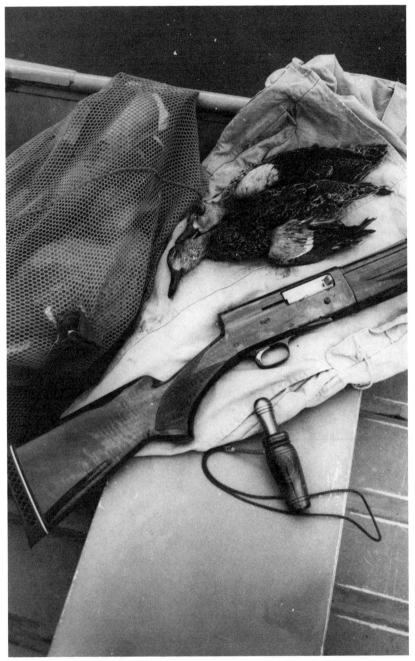

The Browning Auto-5 is a classic favorite among serious waterfowl hunters.

Today, all major firearms makers offer shotguns designed and finished specifically for waterfowl hunters.

er usually eliminates the need for second or third shots.

Another advantage of these specialty guns is their economical price. They are extremely rugged and simple functioning, allowing them to be used in freezing-cold, wet weather. However, their one single biggest disadvantage is the recoil. There is simply nothing to help dampen the recoil, and both these guns from Marlin provide plenty of it.

Double Barrels. A trusty old double was my first waterfowling gun and I still like to shoot with an Ithaca that is twice as old as I am, although I now have to put it aside when using steel shot. Indeed, the double was the traditional waterfowling gun for years and probably accounted for more waterfowl than any other type of gun until the advent of the pumps and semi-automatics.

There are two basic types of double barrels, the traditional side-by-side design and the newer over/under.

Probably the main advantage of the double barrel is the instant choice of chokes. This can be important when your first shot is close-in at decoying mallards, and your next one is a long pass shot at a streaking bluebill.

Another desirable feature of the double is that you can easily break it open to see if it is loaded or to unload it when getting in or out of a blind. By the same token, however, it's a bit awkward to load some of the longer barreled doubles in the blind. This is particu-

Both over/unders and side-by-sides are popular with waterfowl hunters. They have really experienced a resurgence in the last few years.

larly true of the over/unders which must be broken open some distance to push the bottom shell in place. All this can take some doing in the crowded confines of a goose pit.

One disadvantage the side-by-side has to those unaccustomed to shooting one is the wide sighting plane which may seem confusing at first. Raised ribs on the better guns provide help in this area. Of course, the over/under provides the single sighting plane that is easier to use for some.

The first two shots, of course, can be as quick as the first two shots from a pump or automatic. However, you're definitely slowed down in reloading the gun. With practice you can reload a double extremely fast. More than once I've gotten a double with my first two shots and then reloaded and gotten off a third and successful shot at a flight of decoying ducks.

The better double barrels include selective triggers so you can immediately select the barrel you wish to fire, as well as double sighting beads which help to align the target quickly.

Another advantage doubles have is that they are extremely simple in operation and you don't have the maintenance problems that sometimes develop with pumps and especially older autos in cold, wet weather.

A third disadvantage doubles have is their relatively high cost and the fact that few are made in the United States. One exception to this is the Savage Fox. This is an excellent double. I have had one for almost 20 years.

There are also a number of imported doubles as well as several higher grade, more expensive doubles that can be used for waterfowling including the Winchester Models 101 and 21 and the Browning BSS, as well as the Browning Citori and Superposed over/unders. Beretta also makes excellent doubles, as does American Arms. All are chambered for 3-inch magnum shells.

Single Shots. There are a few single shot, breech loading guns on the market including the most famous: the Savage 12 gauge with 32-inch full choke barrel.

The main advantage of these guns is their economical price and the fact that they are easy to load and unload, although breaking down the action can be a hassle in a crowded duck blind. The single sighting plane is also an advantage.

The biggest disadvantage is their "kick." These guns simply have no way to disperse recoil and align the kick dead center on your shoulder! No doubt these are the hardest kicking guns.

Black Powder. There is a growing interest in shooting waterfowl

With the right loads, a muzzleloader can make a fun and challenging waterfowl hunting shotgun. These Canadas are proof that black powder can do the job.

with black powder and as a result there are also a number of black powder shotguns on the market that are ideal for waterfowling. One I have shot quite a bit is the Dixie Double Barrel 12 gauge. They also have a 10 gauge, but I found the 12 to be quite adequate even for big Canada geese. It holds a good pattern out to 50 yards and can be used on ducks or geese.

Black powder shooters quickly find that each gun shoots best with a particular load and I found my best load is two ounces of Number 2 shot over 90 grains of FFG black powder for geese. For ducks I use 1 1/2 ounces of Number 6 shot over 80 grains of powder. If you haven't tried black powder waterfowling you're in for some real fun and excitement and a heck of a challenge!

Choosing The Gauge

Waterfowling guns come in all gauges from .410 to the big 10 gauge. I've seen a few of each in blinds. However, the most common gauges are the 20 and the 12, with the 12 gauge by far the most popular.

With today's modern loads the 20 gauge can be just as efficient a waterfowling gun as the 12 at close to medium ranges. Its lighter weight and smaller dimensions can be an advantage to women and other lightweight hunters. It also provides less recoil, something that can improve the shooting ability of other hunters as well.

It's a good idea to first consider the hunting situation in which you will be using the gun. If long range pass shooting at refuge geese is your bag, then definitely the 12 gauge magnum or perhaps even the 10 gauge might be your logical choice. If you intend to do most of your hunting for decoying mallards and maybe some goose hunting, then the 12 gauge magnum is the best choice. However, if you like to hunt mallards as well as upland game such as quail, you would be better off with a fairly lightweight, short-barreled 12 gauge or even a comparable 20.

I will say that although I've seen a lot of ducks tumbled by 20 gauge shooters, they've all been by experts. I certainly won't knock the 20 as a waterfowling gun. However, in the best interest of making good, clean killing shots and to lessen the chances of wounding and crippling birds, I would suggest a 12 gauge for the average hunter, especially a beginning hunter, who may need a bit of extra edge when first learning how to shoot.

Choosing The Choke

After determining the type of gun and the bore or gauge

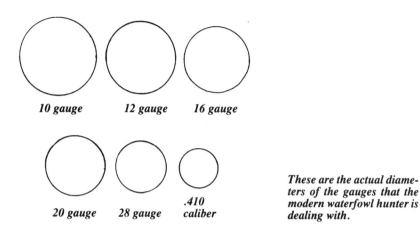

10 gauge   12 gauge   16 gauge

20 gauge   28 gauge   .410 caliber

These are the actual diameters of the gauges that the modern waterfowl hunter is dealing with.

preferred, the next choice you have to make is the choke you want. There have probably been more arguments about choke choices than any other gun subject. One thing even old-timers often forget is that choke determines at what distance the shotgun will be the most effective. Choke is a constriction in the last 1 1/2 inches of the barrel that controls the spread of the shot after it leaves the gun. You can easily compare the nozzle on the end of a water hose to the choke of a shotgun barrel. This spread of the shot is called the pattern.

There are four basic chokes which can be applied to a gun: *Full,* which is the tightest; *modified; improved cylinder;* and *cylinder bore,* which is basically a gun without any choke. A full choke forces the shot charge close together as it leaves the gun, delaying the tendency of the shot to spread. This causes a full choke gun to be more effective at greater distances. At close range, however, such as when hunting close-in decoying ducks, a full choke pattern may be so small that you may have trouble hitting the target or the pattern may be so dense that you destroy the game if you make a direct hit.

According to the old-timers, "If you can't drop a dime down the barrel of a 12 gauge, it's probably just about right." Full choke is usually most effective up to ranges of 50 yards. Modified at 25 to 45, and improved cylinder at 30 to 35 yards.

Although there simply is no perfect choice for all around waterfowling, a modified choke is probably the best choice for the "one-gun" waterfowler who does some decoying work as well as some pass shooting at geese. Of course, with a double barrel waterfowling gun you can literally have your cake and eat it too, with one barrel a

Full choke is the most constricted and keeps the shot closest together.

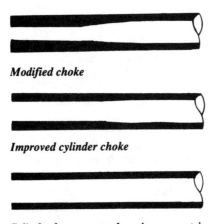

Modified choke

Improved cylinder choke

Cylinder bore means there is no constriction in the barrel and the shot spreads quickly as soon as it leaves the barrel.

These exaggerated drawings show the relative construction of the various degrees of choke commonly found in modern shotguns.

full choke and one a modified. You can use the modified barrel for close-in shots, and save the full choke for those going away or longer distance shots.

There are several alternatives to the single choke gun including an extra barrel that is choked differently and can be changed to suit the hunting situation. Or you can have a Polychoke fitted to your gun by a gunsmith. This is a simple device that can be adjusted in the field to provide the amount of choke you prefer. It takes nothing more than a quick flick of the wrist to set your choke to suit the situation.

A very popular alternative now being offered by most of the gun manufacturers are the choke tubes such as the Invector System by Browning, the Winchoke System by U. S. Repeating Arms Company and the Rem Choke from Remington. These choke systems consist of separate tubes that are threaded to fit into the end of the

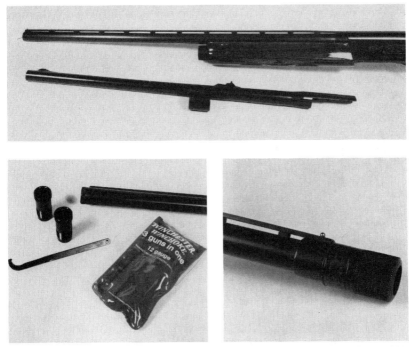

Today's hunter has a number of choices when it comes to changing the choke of his shotgun. He can put on a new barrel, insert a different tube or simply give a special choke device a quick twist.

gun barrel. They can be changed quickly and easily in the field using a small tool made for the purpose, allowing you to match your choke to the hunting situation.

In choosing a choke, consider that in 1991 steel shot will be required for all waterfowl hunting in the United States. Though it loses down range velocity more quickly, steel does tend to pattern more tightly than lead shot. This makes modified chokes even more attractive to the "one gun, one choke" hunter.

Patterning Your Shotgun

Regardless of what type of shotgun you prefer for waterfowling, you must pattern it until you find the right load. If you have a gun with an adjustable choke, this can also be invaluable to determine which of the chokes might be the best for each shooting situation and the actual killing range your gun might have. Patterning your shotgun is easy and a fun excuse for shooting and practicing as well.

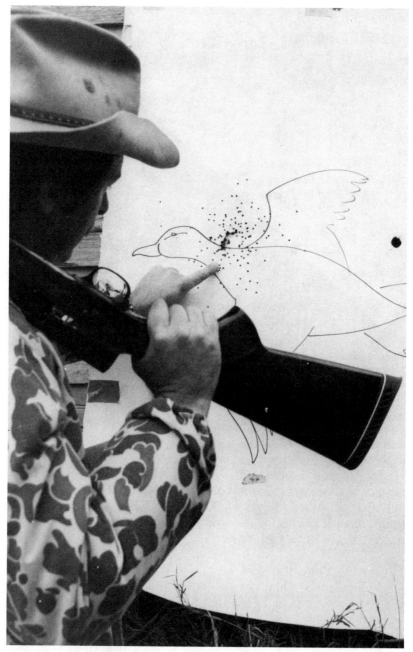

Patterning your shotgun will show you where it shoots and how it handles different loads and shot sizes.

Knowing where and how much shot your shotgun places into a specific area is a very important aspect of good wing shooting. This is done by patterning your gun on a pattern board. A pattern board is made of a piece of four-foot-square, half-inch plywood. It can be made portable by simply leaning it up against a tree, embankment, etc. You can cut it in half and hinge it to make it easier to carry in the trunk of your car. You can also make a permanent board by attaching it to wooden posts driven into the ground. A four foot square piece of paper is thumbtacked to the board for each pattern.

To determine the choke, stand with the muzzle 40 yards from the board and shoot at a large X marked in the center of the board. Draw a 30-inch circle to include the greatest number of shot holes. Count them. The number of shot holes in the circle as opposed to the total number of shot in the charge will provide the percentage and true choke of your gun using that particular load.

Seventy percent or more is a full choke, 50-60 is a modified, 45-50 is an improved cylinder, 30-40 is a true cylinder bore.

Shoot several patterns with a particular load or brand of shotshell, then change. You will find quite a bit of difference, and by testing with the pattern board you can determine the shot size and load, as well as the brand that performs best in your gun.

You can also determine whether the gun shoots to the right, left, up or down, etc., using the pattern board. One fun test is to draw full size profiles of waterfowl and then shoot a pattern on the profile to determine best pattern location on the game for your particular gun and the load chosen.

Remember, the pattern board is not a backstop. You must have an adequate and safe backstop immediately behind the board!

Fitting Your Gun

Unlike a rifle which is ''sighted'' with the aid of a front and back sight, a shotgun is ''pointed'' using your eyes as the back sight. For this reason, to be a consistent wingshooter, the shotgun must come up in place against your body in exactly the same spot and in exactly the same manner each time.

The area where the most adjustment in fit can be made is in the stock. All shotgun stocks are made to fit the ''average'' person (of which none of us are), so to provide a consistent shooting shotgun, you must often alter the shotgun stock to your particular stature and shooting style. For instance, a shotgun with a stock that is too long will slide off a hunter's shoulder onto the arm muscle and can cause bad bruising of the arm. This is frequently a problem with water-

This simple test will reveal if the stock of your shotgun is properly fitted to you.

fowling guns because of the amount of thick and bulky clothing normally worn when hunting.

The simplest method of fitting a gun is to take it to a competent gunsmith and have him do the fitting. However, you can make a couple of quick checks at home to determine if the gun fits properly.

The first is an old traditional method that is still one of the simplest and quickest. Simply place the gun butt in the crook of your arm (wearing your hunting clothing.) The last joint of your first finger should just touch the curve of the trigger. If it doesn't, the stock may need to be lengthened or shortened to suit.

Another simple test you can make at home to determine if the gun comes up properly is to stand in front of a mirror, close your eyes and bring the unloaded gun up into your normal shooting position. Open your eyes. You should be staring at a perfect sight picture. If not, again there may need to be some adjustment to the stock.

Probably the single best thing you can do to determine proper gun fit is to either utilize a ''try stock'' from a local gunsmith or simply try a lot of different guns until you find one that fits and shoots properly for you. Shotgun fit is probably the single most important

The shells you load into your gun are crucial to your shooting success and to the future of the sport.

factor in wing shooting, yet the one that gets the least amount of attention from shooters. By all means make sure you have a recoil pad on your waterfowling gun.

Choosing The Correct Ammunition

Just as choosing the correct shotgun to suit your hunting situation is important, so is choosing the correct ammunition. Geese and ducks have been brought down with everything from a light load of 8's to a heavy load of buckshot, but there are particular loads that are more suited to various types of waterfowling.

When shooting waterfowl, don't scrimp on ammunition. Use only the best, including the shells you load yourself. It takes a lot of power to cut through the heavy layers of down and fat to bring down waterfowl. If you consider that it takes at least a half dozen Number 6 pellets to bring down a mallard, and even more for a big old honker, you can see the requirements.

Most expert waterfowlers prefer to use high-base or magnum shells for ducks and geese. Again the best method is to suit the shotshells to the situation. For instance, when pothole shooting at early season teal, a load of No. 7 ½s will suffice, but when you're trying to pull down a high-flying honker, use the heaviest load you and your gun can stand to insure clean kills and cut down on the chances of crippling.

Indeed, choosing the correct shotshell may seem extremely confusing when you start patterning your gun with the various kinds, particularly if you have a gun with an adjustable choke. Throw in the problems of steel shot and there are more factors involved. However, let's start with lead shot, then handle the problem of steel.

Today's shotshell is made up of a plastic hull, usually with a brass base. Although there are one-piece shells, they're usually used for loads lighter than ones used for waterfowl hunting. The heavier loads usually used for waterfowling have the brass extending higher up on the casing than do the lighter field loads, and for this reason they're usually called "high brass."

The length of the shell is either 2 ¾- or 3-inches. The 3-inch magnums, as they are called, are quite often used for waterfowling because they can contain more powder and shot.

Choosing the correct size and type of shotshell is important. For instance, you can't fire a 3-inch shell in a gun chambered only for 2 ¾-inch shells or in many older guns. However, choosing the correct proportions of the other ingredients is also important. The top of a shotshell box provides the necessary information you need to select the proper shotshell for your particular hunting situation. A typical waterfowl shotshell box might read: *Gauge-12, Inches-3, Dr. Equ 4* (which is the amount of powder) *Oz. shot-1 5/8* (which is the amount of shot) and *Shot-4* (which is the size of the shot.)

The first choice is the size of shot to be used, and this can vary quite a bit with the waterfowl species as well as the hunting situation. The chart shown shows the suggested shot size, choke selection and the average shot in a 30-inch circle at 40 yards. However, this is only average and you will need to pattern your gun with various ammunition to determine the best load for your gun.

Also shown is a chart of the actual sizes of the various shot as well as the number of shot pellets per ounce for both lead and steel.

All manufacturers offer their ammunition in various grades, running basically as shown, with the premier grades offering not only the most ingredients, but extras such as copper plated and buffered shot. Plating the shot with copper hardens the shot so it stays rounder

NO.	9	8½	8	7½	6	5	4	2	1	BB
SHOT SIZES **Diameter** **in inches**	.08	.085	.09	.095	.11	.12	.13	.15	.16	.18

BUCKSHOT **Diameter** **in inches**	No. 4 .24	No. 3 .25	No. 2 .27	No. 1 .30	No. 0 .32	No. 00 .33	No. 000 .36

SHOT PELLETS PER OUNCE (Approximate)

LEAD				STEEL	
Size	Pellets	Size	Pellets	Size	Pellets
BB	50	6	225	BB	72
2	87	7½	350	1	103
4	135	8	410	2	125
5	170	9	585	4	192
				6	315

These charts will aid you in selecting the right loads for your next waterfowl hunting expedition.

BIRD	FLIGHT SPEED	RECOMMENDED SHOT SIZE	CHOKE SELECTION	AVERAGE SHOT IN 30" CIRCLE AT 40 YARDS
Diving Ducks	48–75 mph	4, 5, or 6	Mod-Full	Mod 45–60% Full 65–80%
Puddle Ducks	35–65 mph	4, 5, or 6	Mod-Full	Mod 45–60% Full 65–80%
Geese	45–60 mph	BB, 2, or 4	Full-Full	65–80%

DUCKS
Use no. 4 shot for pass shooting. Use no. 5 or 6 shot for closer shots—for example, over decoys.

GEESE
Goose hunters need a lot of shock to knock down these birds, and so they use big loads and large shot. A gun that throws a dense pattern is extremely important. For average shooting, experienced hunters usually use no. 4 shot.

These are the basic components of any shotshell.

in flight, thus creating a denser, tighter pattern and better performance. By the same token, the addition of buffer compounds such as
polypropylene also provides denser patterns.

The basic progression of grades starts with target loads, which
are the lightest, and running through a variety of field loads, "Express" loads, Magnums, buffered magnums and finally the super
magnums. Shown is a chart from Remington with the information on
their various grades so you can see the comparison. Naturally, the
higher you go in the grades, the more expensive the shotshells become. You may wish to select the lighter "field" loads for the lighter shooting situations such as early-season decoying mallards. However, later in the season you may wish to go to heavier loads such as
Express or even magnums for the same hunting situation when the
ducks have become more wary and more fully feathered. When
hunting for big honkers you might as well figure on taking the best
magnum shotshell you can buy, especially late in the season.

In addition to these basic grades, each manufacturer may also
carry various "lines" that all have these grades. There are differences in price between the lines as well as the "grades."

Steel Shot. Because of the problem of lead poisoning in waterfowl and predatory birds such as eagles, steel shot regulations were
instituted in the 1976-77 season in many areas of the country. Since

Buffered loads prevent the individual pellets from deformation as they slam together while traveling down a shotgun's barrel.

that time there has been a growing number of areas requiring the use of nontoxic or steel shot only, and by 1991, all waterfowl hunters are required to use it. The controversy over the effectiveness of steel shot as a hunting and conservation tool will no doubt continue for years, but most experts agree that it has definitely helped reduce the loss of waterfowl and birds of prey due to lead ingestion.

The biggest problem for waterfowlers is that steel shot simply doesn't act the same as the softer lead shot. Since it isn't as heavy as lead shot, it loses velocity sooner. This means you will have to limit your shots to shorter ranges than with lead. Most experts suggest that no shots should be taken over 40 yards, even with the best steel loads. However, there have been improvements in loads for steel shot from the first experiments and today's steel shot loads are much better than their earlier counterparts.

Some hunters move up to the next larger shot size to compensate for the velocity problems. However, since steel shot deforms less it produces a much tighter pattern than lead shot (at close and medium ranges). So in effect, you can often get a tighter pattern with steel Number 6's than you might have with buffered lead 4's. Number 6

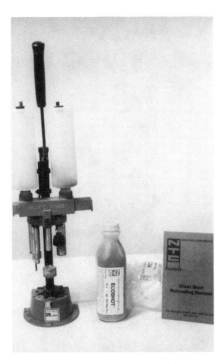

As more data and materials become available, reloading steel shot will be a safe, economical alternative to factory rounds.

shot, whether lead or steel is a good shot choice when hunting over decoys.

Shot Stringing. The last thing to throw into the picture is the effect of shot stringing. It affects both steel and lead, although steel to a lesser degree.

A paper pattern of your shot will reveal the amount of shot pellets in a circle or target at certain distances, but not all shot reaches the pattern or target at the same time due to minute differences in pellet weight and pellet deformation caused by set- back and/or barrel scrub.

The shot is actually in the form of a string, which means that only some of your shot may effectively hit where you intend, while some of the late arriving shot may in effect hit farther back on a moving target than would show on a stationary pattern target. Steel shot doesn't string as much as lead, which means hunters must lead their targets more precisely because the chances of them flying into the middle of string is reduced.

Reloading

Good waterfowling shotshells are expensive and the cost of steel shells can be exorbitant, sometimes running well over $15 a box. Many waterfowlers like to cut expenses by reloading shells, which often allows them to load a ''better'' shell than they might be able to afford if purchased. Reloading can be fun and relaxing as well.

At this writing, the number of components for reloading steel shells is increasing and should continue to increase as steel shot regulations tighten to the 1991 total compliance requirement. This is good news for reloaders who in the past have had trouble finding steel shot components and reloading manuals.

Many old blind designs like this pit have been made more comfortable and durable through the use of space age materials in their construction.

5

Blinds:
Simple To Space Age

A waterfowling blind can be as simple as a piece of canvas used to cover hunters lying in a field, or as elaborate as a plywood "shack" complete with roof and gas heat.

Both types, and anything in between for that matter, can be successful if they meet three requirements: 1)*A blind must conceal the hunters.* 2)*It must blend in naturally with the surroundings.* 3)*It must be located in an area that is used by waterfowl.*

One of the most successful blinds I have ever shot from consisted of nothing more than a few tree branches stuck in the soft mud on a point of an island on a large reservoir. The blind was accessible by boat only. Each hunter brought along a stool or bucket to sit on. The shooting was absolutely fantastic through the first part of the season, until the leaves began to drop from the branches of the blind, as well as the nearby trees.

On the other hand, one of the most elaborate blinds I have ever visited was on a private lake in Arkansas. It was two stories tall, with cook shack and bunkhouse on the bottom floor, and shooting blind on the top floor! Completely heated, and with all the comforts of home, the top shooting portion had a drop down hinged "window" that was opened when it came time to shoot.

There are, however, basically just three different types of blinds; permanent, semi-permanent, and portable. As you can guess, there are many different kinds of blinds in each of these categories.

Permanent blinds are those that are constructed for season after season of use at a single site. Examples include concrete pit blinds, stake blinds and some wooden box blinds.

Semi-permanent blinds are movable, but generally left in one location for a season or a good portion of a season. These include boat blinds, floating blinds that can be pulled up on land, and blinds on skids that are also pulled into position.

Portable blinds also consist of boats, which we will discuss in the next chapter, and a number of small, light-weight blinds that may be moved easily from one spot to another. Portable blinds also include the various types of camouflage cloth that can be used to make a temporary blind almost anywhere the birds are flying.

Permanent Above Ground Blinds

These blinds may be located over the water, or on land next to a slough, lake or marsh. For the most part these are usually made of wood. Rough-sawn hardwood is the best choice because it will weather to a natural color that blends with the surroundings, and it is tough enough to withstand the elements, insects, etc. Some permanent above ground blinds are constructed from poured concrete.

Above Water. One of the most common permanent blinds is the

A blind built on pilings above water is sturdy and comfortable!

No matter what type of permanent blind you're hunting from, location is key.

stake blind that is positioned over the water in shallow bays or lakes. These are usually built on pilings or stakes driven or sunken into the bottom of the lake or bay. They are quite common in some portions of the Southern coasts.

There are advantages in that they provide a great deal of comfort and safety, however, because they're permanently anchored to terra firma, they can't be repositioned if necessary to follow waterfowl movements. Although waterfowl do use traditional routes, they can often be quite fickle as well. One day you can have fabulous shooting from a permanent blind, and the next a complete bomb.

A similar type of blind, also used in the South, is a tree blind, made by fastening a platform in the top of a huge tree, much in the fashion of a kid's playhouse. These can be extremely effective in other areas too, but be sure to check if they're legal in the area you hunt before building one.

The second type of permanent blinds are those built on the ground or shore. These can consist of almost anything, however, they are most commonly made of wood, and in the shape of an open fronted box. They are usually then covered with natural camouflage.

These blinds can also be constructed with a concrete floor and shell, or positioned on pilings, etc.

Sunken, Pit Or Below Ground Blinds

Probably the single most effective type of blind for both ducks and geese is the sunken, or pit blind. Again this can be an elaborate affair, or simply a hole dug in the ground to conceal the hunter or hunters.

Goose Pits. Of the most common sunken blinds are the goose pits used by commercial guides and goose hunting operations. These are made in several different ways and using a number of different types of materials.

One of the simplest methods, and one that affords a ready-made blind quite easily is a discarded metal tank. It must be at least a 500-gallon tank to be able to hold two or more hunters comfortably. The top may be cut off, and a hinged wooden cover provided, or a portion of the top may be left on, cutting only a quarter section from the front and top. Holes are bored in the bottom to provide rain water drainage, and wooden benches and shelves are bolted in place.

These blinds are fairly "portable" in that they can be removed after each season and then positioned in the best "feed field" just before the next season. This does of course require the use of a heavy-duty tractor equipped for digging and hauling the blind, but it is an extremely effective method of creating a blind in the best goose feeding fields each season. In some cases this type of blind is left in the ground permanently, with the farmer plowing around them during planting time.

Constructed properly, these can be the most comfortable blinds in the country, even in freezing drizzle or snow.

Goose pits are often constructed of wood, creating an open framework of two-by-fours to hold the seats, dog boxes, etc. These are also usually equipped with a wooden cover. The most effective ones have a hinged, camouflaged cover that can be thrown back for shooting. Pit blinds are constructed most easily above ground (then lowered into the hole dug for them), but the blind can also be built inside the hole. The latter is, however, much more difficult to construct.

One of the most effective pit blinds I have ever been in was a small hole just big enough for two people to hunker in, located in the middle of a half picked field of corn. We had been watching geese avoid our permanent pit blind for almost a week when we finally decided to make a move.

This well-constructed blind will accommodate a number of hunters and do a good job in concealing them from wary geese.

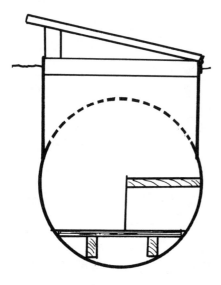

A well-constructed pit blind offers the ultimate in comfort.

It didn't take two guys very long to dig the hole, complete with "shelf" to sit on. We simply pulled a camouflage cloth over our heads, along with a few corn stalks, and had some of the best shooting I've ever experienced on big, old Canada honkers.

Sunken Blinds. Sunken blinds of various construction can also be quite effective for hunting ducks. Again, one of the most productive duck blinds I've hunted from was nothing more than a small hole I could slide into off a windy spit of land reaching a half mile out into a large reservoir.

Most permanent sunken blinds used for ducks are quite a bit more elaborate. These are normally permanently located as opposed to the more mobile goose pits. Marshes, lakes and other areas that ducks traditionally frequent are used more consistently than the feed fields of geese, which can change each week. Again, a metal barrel can be used to create a blind, much in the same manner as for goose pits, however the most common method of installing an in-ground duck blind is to pour one of concrete. This may have a poured concrete top or the top may be wooden framework covered with rough sawn hardwood boards, then camouflaged each season.

I have spent many comfortable mornings ensconced in such a blind, owned by Judge Kelso of southwestern Missouri. Located in the middle of a couple thousand acres of flooded river bottoms, with

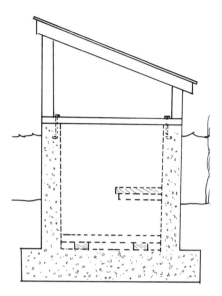

Sunken blinds built of poured concrete can be built in areas that are annually flooded.

a small pool in front of it, the blind provides some of the best and last "green timber" mallard hunting in the country.

The blind is constructed so the water level, at normal pool, comes just about six inches below the top of the blind. Sitting in the blind you are below water level, and when a couple hundred mallards decide to come in, they just barrel down almost on top of you. This grand old blind regularly produces some unusual and exciting hunting.

Of course, the blind has to be bailed often when the river, which makes a big bend around the timbered bottom lands, gets too high. The blind is well over 30 years old, and still provides some mighty comfortable and exciting shooting. The top of the blind consists of a log frame work over which sheet metal roofing has been applied, then logs, brush and other natural camouflage materials added.

In most instances concrete blinds are constructed on site because of the weight involved. This consists of creating an inside and outside form, in much the same manner as pouring the basement of a house. The form must also be well reinforced to withstand the pressure of water and earth around it. After the form is constructed and reinforcing added, the concrete is mixed, poured and allowed to cure. Then the surrounding area is back-filled around it to the correct depth, etc.

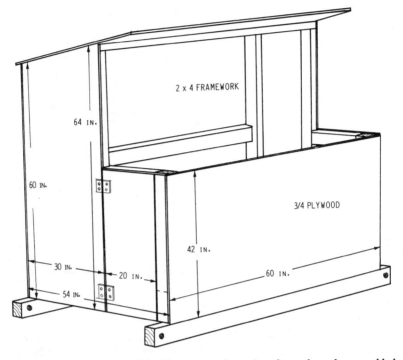

2 x 4 FRAMEWORK

64 IN.

60 IN.

3/4 PLYWOOD

42 IN.

30 IN.

20 IN.

54 IN.

60 IN.

This blind, constructed with 2x4 framing and exterior plywood can be assembled at home then towed into position on runners or foam flotation.

One of the biggest problems that occurs with these blinds is that they will sometimes "float" if they remain flooded permanently. The best location for them is an area that is flooded each season.

These blinds can be located out in the open with water surrounding them. Quite often they are also positioned in the berm, dike or bank of a lake. When positioned in this manner, a door is often placed in the back for easy entry into the blind.

Camouflaging these blinds is fairly easy. One good method is to plant wild roses or vining plants around them. Otherwise, simply pile native vegetation around them.

Semi-Permanent Blinds

Floating Blinds. Floating blinds share many of the same features of the permanent in-ground blinds. They also range from nothing

Many floating blinds allow you to drive the boat right inside!

more than a small platform to huge houses that hunters can sleep, eat and practically live in through the season. The one thing that separates them, however, is portability. Floating blinds can be moved to follow the ducks, making them superior to permanent blinds in some instances. Floating blinds are not to be confused with boat blinds, which will be discussed in the next chapter although many of them have space to position a boat inside or under them.

The simplest floating blind is a wooden platform supported by dock floats, or similar flotation materials. In many cases a wooden framework is also constructed on the platform to which camouflage materials can be fastened. The blind is floated to the location and anchored. Hunters reach the blind by wading or boat. Another method of using these blinds is to tow them to a hard-to-get-to land location, then push them up on land to locate them for the season.

John Magnum, owner of Bucksaw Point Marina on Truman Lake in Central Missouri, has several of these blinds set up for his commercial waterfowl hunting operation. They are wooden platforms built on light-weight aluminum pontoons. A metal framework covered with camouflaged canvas provides a comfortable, easy-to-shoot-from blind and shelter, complete with heater, cookstove and

For safety sake, hunters must put thought and effort into the construction of a big floating blind.

plenty of room for guide and hunters.

Dell Arduser, a duck hunting guide and close friend with whom I have hunted for several years, also favors a floating blind, and he probably builds the best in the country. His blinds are the typical platform on flotation, but with one major difference. The platform has a hole cut in the center for a boat, and the blind is open on one end so the boat can be driven in. The blind is anchored before the season on traditional duck flyways of Truman Lake. It has space for a heater, and provides plenty of comfort for as many as four hunters. Hunters actually shoot out of the boat.

The technique is to drive the boat inside the blind. Wooden planks are brought down over the gunwales of the boat and fastened to both the front and back of the blind platform. This anchors the boat securely in place. Cushions are then placed on these planks providing a comfortable easy-to-see-out seating arrangement. To shoot, gunners simply stand up in the boat. Dell continues to refine his blinds. They seem to get larger. Even though I kidded him about the improbability of his most recent "barges" floating, they have provided some fantastic hunting, and have been mighty comfortable during sleet and freezing rain.

A well-constructed and properly anchored floating blind provides a safe and comfortable hunting site even in the worst weather.

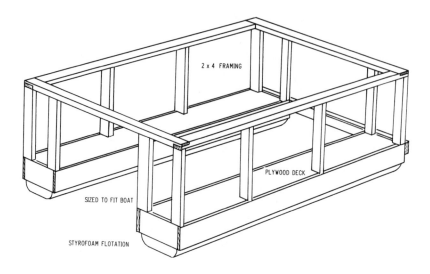

2 x 4 FRAMING

PLYWOOD DECK

SIZED TO FIT BOAT

STYROFOAM FLOTATION

A good floating blind starts with solid construction from the frame out.

Although most floating blinds are constructed of wood framing, Dell's are made of pipe, welded together. A sheetmetal roof and back cut down on the wind and weather, and provide a comfortable, snug blind.

Dell hunts on a Corps of Engineer lake which requires that blinds be removed within 10 days of the close of each season, and in the past he used a pontoon boat trailer to load, haul and launch his blinds. Recently, however, due to the huge size of his latest blinds, he has had to build a special trailer to launch them. The custom rig works like a charm. In fact, it works more efficiently than using the pontoon boat trailer did in the past.

Be aware, there is some danger in using floating blinds particularly if they are built too top heavy. Dell has seen several blinds similar to his, constructed by other hunters in the area, flip over or swamp. To reduce the chance of this happening, make sure they are securely anchored in place from all directions.

Coffin Blinds. Coffin blinds are just as they sound, a small wooden box that can be partially buried to conceal a single hunter. They are usually constructed of lightweight marine plywood. Many are also waterproofed so they can be towed behind a boat as a ''decoy tender.'' After the decoys are set, the ''blind'' is positioned in shallow water or placed in a shallow pit and covered with natural camouflage.

Although they are not the most comfortable or conducive to companionship, coffin blinds can be extremely effective, especially on the heavily pressured, wary ducks of larger lakes or reservoirs. They are usually located on an island or spit of land on the traditional waterfowl routes of the area.

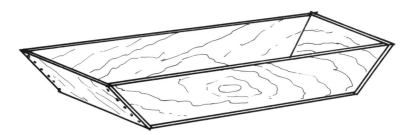

A homemade coffin blind is simple and effective.

Barrel Blind. Quite similar in both use and construction, a barrel blind is a section of either a metal or wooden barrel that is partially buried in the ground. It is about as comfortable as a coffin blind, except in the former you lie down, and in the barrel you must squat. Both can be quite awkward for shooting, and uncomfortable after a time. Like the coffin blind, however, it is an extremely effective blind for wary waterfowl.

Mirror Blinds

One of the most effective and unusual blinds I have ever used was designed by Bill Harper, president of Lohman Game Call Company, and an old hunting friend. The blind was a small four-sided box of Masonite panels covered with mirrored Mylar. It was used in a goose feeding field, was light-weight and portable enough to be moved quite easily to the best feeding areas. Although made primarily for one man, it could be made larger in size to accommodate more than one.

Although construction of the blind is fairly easy, it does take some unusual materials. The ''mirror'' is actually mirrored Mylar, a plastic material that is available from solar heating supply

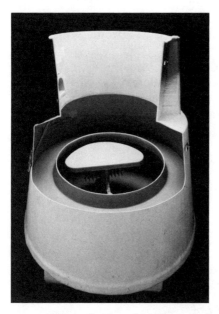

The old barrel blind has been made more portable, comfortable and durable through the use of modern materials.

companies. It is glued to light-weight wooden or tempered hardboard panels with waterproof glue. Wooden corner strengtheners are glued in place over the ends of all four panels. These are simply bolted together using lag bolts and wing nuts when you locate a spot to hunt.

Although it sounds "space age," and like an idea that would be scoffed at by waterfowling traditionalists, the blind simply disappears when erected!

Position it in a feed field that geese are using, along with several decoys around it, and geese will practically land in your lap!

Portable Blinds

These days mobility is often the key to successful waterfowl hunting. This is due to changing land use, more pressure from hunters, and fewer ducks and geese in traditional hunting areas. The answer is a small portable blind that can be carried easily to the most remote places, and set up quickly and easily.

There are any number of these blinds available, ranging from nothing more than a special perforated "army" type camouflage cloth that can be thrown over hunters, to specially designed "tent" type blinds that have a pop-up lid. The latter are usually made as one-man blinds and will completely conceal a hunter quite effectively. When the hunter has a shot, he simply flips back the top or lid and

The most portable of blinds is simply a bolt of camouflage fabric or netting strung between two stakes pounded into the ground.

raises up to shoot. Most of these blinds require the shooter to squat or sit and for this reason a small light-weight stool can provide a great deal of added comfort.

You can also build your own portable blinds using a handful of aluminum stakes and a roll of camouflage material. Fasten the stakes to the camouflage material by sewing pieces of Velcro in the positions you wish the poles to be. To use, merely push into the ground in a semi-circle around you. These can also be used to enlarge a blind when you have a group of hunters and need extra camouflage.

Some hunters take the camo fabric route a step farther by creating their own natural camouflage covers. They weave natural covers like corn stalks, wheat stems or cattails into chicken wire. The size of these panels can vary from small for covering a single hunter lying in a field to huge for covering large fishing boats!

Locating Blinds

Regardless of how well constructed or camouflaged the blind is, unless it is situated in an area used by waterfowl it will be useless. In most instances waterfowl tend to use traditional routes, resting and feeding areas to some degree. This is particularly so of resting areas, although feeding areas may change according to the availability of food in the area.

Weather and the progress of the harvest are two important variables that affect feeding areas and thus blind placement.

In instances of private hunting clubs and lakes, blind spots are fairly well established. But when hunting the open water, large lakes or public lakes and marshes, placement of a portable or movable blind can dictate the success of a day, or even a season. In this instance, prehunt scouting is necessary. This can be done before the season, and is especially effective when locating resting areas.

Keep in mind that feeding and resting areas can change a great deal during the course of a season, and the hunter who can stay mobile to follow the most waterfowl flights will be the most successful.

Position of the blind is extremely important for different species. Goose blinds are usually located in known feed fields such as harvested corn, soybeans, or winter wheat. Puddle duck blinds are usually situated on land near traditional waterfowl use areas. All ducks, however, prefer not to fly over land, so the best blind locations are the lee points of islands, or narrow points of land that run out into open water.

Locating a blind on a small pothole or marsh is not as complicated because most waterfowl have a traditional route into and out of the area. Knowing where they will come from, such as a nearby refuge or large river, allows you to place the blind for the best shooting. If possible, blinds should be located with their backs to the prevailing wind. All waterfowl like to land against the wind, and this allows them to land in front of you rather than surprising you from the back. It also provides the most shelter from the weather. By the same token, locating a blind facing the morning or evening sun can create a terrible shooting situation, so that should also be considered.

Blind Camouflage

Proper camouflaging of the blind is important. It should be done well in advance of the season, if the blind is permanently located. Regardless of all else, the camouflage must match the surroundings. Natural camouflage is the best bet, and anything from marsh hay or grass to tree limbs work depending on the situation. Most public hunting areas, however, require that you do not cut native vegetation for building blinds, in which case you will need to take your blind camouflage along with you. Again homemade or store- bought camo covers are excellent for that purpose.

6

Waterfowling Boats:
Tradition & Today

B oats are almost a necessity for waterfowlers. Some waterfowlers
may have good hunting spots that can be reached by land without the use of a boat, but for the most part, boats are an important part of many waterfowlers' gear. Just about anything can and probably has been used as a waterfowling boat. Many boats also double as fishing as well as hunting boats. There are, however, some specialized boats that are used only for waterfowling. Waterfowling boats may be used only to transport hunters to and from a blind, or they may serve as the blind as well.

Regardless of what type of boat is used, it must serve one important purpose; it must efficiently haul hunters, dogs and gear to and from hunting spots safely in every hunting situation in which it is used. A boat needed to haul a couple of hunters through sheltered waters of flooded timber is definitely not the same boat that is needed to haul a couple hundred decoys, several hunters, dogs and other gear across several miles of open water in blustery weather. Regardless of all else, the boat must be seaworthy to suit the situation. Many waterfowl hunters have died or have had harrowing experiences when using a too small or improper craft, or simply trying to hunt in weather that was too dangerous. Know your boat, and its capabilities.

There is no duck or goose in this world that's worth dying for! Use common sense on the water!

Any ordinary fishing boat can be put into service as a transport boat for the waterfowl hunter. With a bit of camouflaging skill, it can even make a tolerable hunting blind.

Transport Boats

Again, almost anything that is safe enough to use in the particular water situation can be used as a transport boat. The ordinary "jon boat" is quite often used to haul hunters to and from a blind. Even a bass boat can often be used, if you carry along a camouflage cover for it.

Boat Blinds

One of the most effective and mobile methods of hunting waterfowl on inland reservoirs or lakes is a boat blind. This is simply a boat that has built-in camouflage or is shaped so camouflage can be fitted over it to create a "blind." There are several manufactured varieties available, or you can create your own.

In practically all instances the "blind" portion consists of steel, aluminum or plastic tubing shaped to create an overhead blind which is covered with natural or manufactured camouflage materials. There are almost as many different varieties of camouflage covers as there are waterfowlers, and many are quite ingenious.

One problem that often happens with boat blinds is that they can easily become top heavy and dangerous. Two hunters drowned on a lake near my home a couple years ago hunting out of such a rig. They were caught by high winds and the boat simply rolled over.

Camouflaging Your Fishing Boat

Quite often a fishing boat can be camouflaged as a duck boat/blind. This also includes bass boats. John Gleason, a fellow outdoor writer and duck hunting buddy also guides fishermen on Table Rock Lake in Missouri. He uses his bass boat for duck hunting, and has rigged a quite ingenious blind that fits his boat. One advantage he has is that his bass boat is brown and cream colored Fiberglas, and not particularly flashy. He has simply made plastic pipe frames which fit down into holes in wooden blocks clamped to the gunwales of his boat. The frames extend up on both sides of the boat and are covered with mesh camouflage material. It is extremely effective, and allows him to simply remove the side frames to again use his boat for fishing.

Butch Lawson, a duck hunting guide and friend, has one of the simplest boat blinds I've ever seen. It is one of the earliest bass boats, with an open cockpit, rather than decked over. Two fishing

There are numerous ways to conceal boats and make blinds of them. Shown is a plastic pipe frame covered with wire and natural camouflage.

The special panels rigged on this fishing boat turn it into a fine duck hunting blind.

seats are fastened into place in the boat, and it is equipped with a front-mounted trolling motor. Butch has painted the entire boat in camouflage, matching the pattern to the surroundings of the lakes he hunts. The pattern looks like upright trees and brush. Everything on the boat is painted in that manner, including the motor and trolling motor. When shoved up against a treeline, the boat becomes almost invisible, even to the human eye.

I've seen mallards come within a dozen yards of both of us sitting out in the open in the boat. According to Butch, "As long as you don't move, they'll come right in."

You can also paint your own boat in a pattern to suit the terrain of the area you hunt. Make sure you use paint that is suited to your boat. For instance, aluminum requires different paint than Fiberglas. Choose only good quality camouflage paints from outdoor supply companies.

One interesting aspect of Butch's boat is his use of the trolling motor. He finds it much easier to control the boat while setting out

Be sure to pay special attention to shiny and brightly colored areas of your boat when you're turning it into a hunting blind.

and retrieving decoys by using the trolling motor instead of his · outboard.

If you don't want to paint your fishing boat, one of the simplest methods of camouflaging it is to use one of the manufactured covers. The best are the ''army'' style that are perforated and appear like ''leaves.'' The better ones are green camo on one side and brown on the other. They can quickly be thrown over a boat to create an instant ''blind.''

Specialty Waterfowling Boats

Waterfowling boats have become a tradition throughout the country, and the century. They range from the poled cypress jon boats of the South, to the layout boats of the open bays, to the Barnegat Bay Sneak Box of the Jersey Coast. Regardless, they all have one thing in common, they are designed primarily for waterfowling, and each is specifically suited to its type of waterfowl hunting. Today there is a resurgence of interest in many of these traditional waterfowling boats. The increase in public hunting on the growing numbers of large reservoirs is one reason.

Barnegat Bay Sneak Box. Probably the most famous waterfowling boat of all is the Barnegat Bay Sneak Box. It originated in the early 1800s and was designed and constructed by Captain Sea-

This is a modern version of the Barnegat Bay sneak box. Photo courtesy of Windswept Gunning Skiffs.

man, from Barnegat Bay, New Jersey. It was used extensively by market gunners of the period and was an excellent craft for gunning the tidal sound, even in rough weather. It is designed to both row and sail and has a low profile which makes it an ideal open water shooting boat.

The Barnegat Bay Sneak Box was actually a completely self-contained unit. The boat's design was so efficient that it could be used as a sculling boat, a layout boat for open water, or as a sneak boat for the marshes. It was easily concealed on open water or in marsh vegetation.

The original design was a clean, round bottom, seaworthy craft. With the advent of the outboard motor, the design gradually changed to adapt to gasoline power. The boats became bigger, the sides became higher and there were, of course, outboard motor brackets on the transom. It must be remembered, however, that the sneak box was basically a "type" of boat rather than a single design, and there were numerous versions and styles.

Today there is a resurgence of interest in the sneak box waterfowling boat. Several different companies are now manufacturing it, in several different styles.

Probably the most true to form copy of the original is being hand built by Geoff Matthews, a hunting guide and manager of the Amherst Wildlife Foundation of Ontario, Canada. Like the original, it is made to be rowed or sailed. Mathews' boat does not take an outboard motor. The boat construction is a combination of traditional wooden boat building techniques and Fiberglas. It has a one-piece Fiberglas hull with a one-piece Fiberglas deck fitted in place. It has white oak runners, skeg and cockpit coaming, as well as removable white oak floor boards. There is a traditional canvas spray curtain that is fastened in place with snaps. The boat is completely decked over except for the cockpit, and there is a decoy rack which fits on the back deck to hold decoys.

Because each boat is hand-built, it can be custom designed to suit the hunter. This includes installing a sculling port in the transom rack to transform the boat into a sculling rig.

There are also a number of modern versions of the sneak box that are designed to accept outboard motors. These range in size from a tiny 11-footer to a big 20-footer that will carry three hunters, dogs and all their gear.

Sculling Boats. These were also a popular waterfowling craft on the East Coast during the market hunting days, and there are still a few of them around. They were also called "sneak boats" because of their intended purpose—they were used to sneak up on rafts of ducks on open water. A hole in the transom allowed a hunter to scull (row with a single oar) the boat toward the unsuspecting waterfowl.

Most of these boats were made to accommodate two men, the sculler and the shooter. The boats were shallow draft and usually had a screen across their bow to further camouflage the hunters laying in the bottom of the boat. Once the boat was in range of the rafting waterfowl, the gunners would sit up and shoot. The front gunner shot to the front and one side, the sculler would shoot at any birds coming around behind the boat.

Sculling rigs were usually quite well camouflaged, sometimes with cedar limbs and driftwood tied on to make the boat resemble a drift of debris. Sometimes a carved gull decoy was also place on the boat as a confidence builder. Quite often sneak boxes were rigged as sculling boats. Almost any type of low-profile fishing boat could be set up in the same manner.

Another use of the rig was to make a fairly large set of decoys in open water and watch it from shore. Once it had attracted a raft of ducks, then again a sneak was made.

Layout Boat. A layout boat is quite similar to the "battery" or

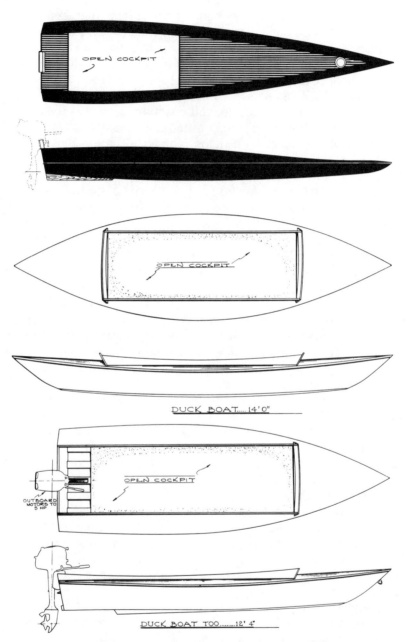

These detailed drawings show the shape and relative dimensions of modernized duck boat designs. The top is from a sculling rig background.

The modern specialty duck boat, often based on traditional designs, fills the widest variety of waterfowling situations.

sinkbox boats. In the latter, however the gunner sits below water level.

A layout boat is also of extremely shallow draft and flat and allows the gunner to lay just about at water level. It is a highly efficient, and most exciting and challenging method of hunting.

Layout boats are used in the open waters of large lakes, and bays with huge sets of decoys, to create an artificial ''raft'' of ducks. Layout boats are like battery and sinkboxes, illegal in some areas or states, so check with local authorities before using one.

In most instances a layout boat is quite small, just enough space for one man. With a spread of decoys around the boat, they're almost impossible to see. They are usually about four feet wide, eight feet long, and about 18 inches deep, shaped like a flat ''pumpkin seed''—another common name for the layout boat. In heavy seas a canvas spray apron is spread out from the boat to dampen the waves and make the rig's camouflage even more efficient.

Because of the size and shape of the layout boat it is rarely used for transportation to or from a hunting site. Normally a second larger boat is used to tow the layout boat into position, with the layout boat being used as a decoy tender during transportation to and from the hunting area. Then the layout boat is set up with the decoys and the transportation boat located some distance away. The hunters take turns shooting from the layout boat and retrieving birds with the transport boat. It makes for exciting, highly productive shooting.

There are some layout boats on the market, or you could make your own. Shown are the general dimensions for an old-time layout boat.

Punts. A chapter on waterfowling boats would not be complete without mentioning the double-end punts that were famous on the East Coast during the days of market gunners. Extremely seaworthy, these traditional waterfowling boats often doubled as fishing skiffs. There are still some builders creating these hand-made waterfowling traditions in local areas.

Other Boats As Waterfowling Rigs

Canoes. Many hunters don't think of canoes as a good waterfowling boat, and of course, they should not be used on rough open water. But they can be used on protected waters quite effectively. One of the most productive ways to hunt during the early season is to slip down a creek or river, jump-shooting mallards or black ducks that are resting on the quiet, secluded back waters.

Almost any canoe can be used, but it should be stable and large

The collapsible Porta-Bote is a good option for the hunter who doesn't have the space to store a regular boat during the off season.

Other waterfowling "boat" options are the innertube, canoe or inflatable raft. All work extremely well under specific conditions.

enough to accommodate the hunter or hunters. It helps to have a dull colored or camouflaged canoe, however, a piece of camo cloth can be thrown over the bow to help cut down any flash or bright colors. The most important factor in a successful canoe hunt, however, is stealth. The trick is to slip down the river as quietly as possible. Stay to the inside edge of the bank as you approach a turn that may have a pool of quiet water behind it. And be prepared for some fast and exciting shooting at flushing birds. Paddle quietly and carefully! The wise mallards who have left the noise and crowds of the big public hunting areas won't sit still for a canoe paddle banging off an aluminum hull!

For safety sake most canoe hunters only allow the front gunner to shoot, while the back hunter paddles and guides the canoe. The hunters switch back and forth to give each other a chance to shoot.

Portable Boats. Many waterfowlers don't have the space to keep a full-size boat, even a jon boat. Nor do they have a vehicle large enough to haul one. The answer is a portable boat.

There are several on the market, but one I found extremely good for waterfowling is the Porta-Bote. One model is manufactured in a dark green. The 12-foot size is plenty big enough for one or two hunters, dog and all the gear. It folds down flat and can be tied to the top of a small car, camper, etc. To set up, merely pop out the sides, install the seats, and you're ready for action. The boats come with oarlocks, but will handle outboards up to 7.5 horsepower. They weigh just 59 pounds, and fold down to four flat inches.

Inflatables. There are also several inflatables on the market that make excellent waterfowling boats for those short on storage or hauling space. One of the best is the Sea Eagle Model 9 which will accommodate two hunters, dogs and gear. It has wooden floor boards for strength and will take up to a four horsepower motor. It is ideal for getting around in sheltered waters, and takes up little space when not inflated. It is available in green and is easily camouflaged.

Innertubing For Ducks

A relatively new type of duck hunting has developed on many of the inland lakes and public duck hunting marshes; the use of a floating, fishing innertube rig for duck hunting. It does provide some extremely exciting and productive hunting, and allows a hunter to hunt some areas that might not be accessible otherwise. It's especially good for hunting green timber areas that might have deep holes in them, causing wading hunters problems.

Innertubing does allow a hunter to walk into a public hunting area, particularly on one of the reservoirs, while carrying a couple dozen decoys and the tube. He can then use the tube to position decoys in water deeper than he could wade, and shoot from the bank, using the tube to retrieve waterfowl. Other hunters like to shoot from the tube, but it does take practice. Swinging on and connecting with birds is a whole new thrill when shooting from a tippy tube!

Of course the tube should only be used in back waters or protected areas away from heavy seas. A pair of swim flippers or special feet wings made for use with the tube can be used to help propel the hunter.

Hunting from a rubber ''donut'' is not easy, but it can be extremely productive in out-of-the-way areas, and provide the waterfowler with another method of scoring on today's hard-to-hunt birds. Because of the increasing popularity of tube hunting many manufacturers of the outfits are now selling them with camouflage covers. You can also simply throw a mesh camouflage cover over yourself and the tube to provide plenty of camouflage. The hunter can situate himself directly in the center of the decoy set when tube hunting, much like the hunter in a layout boat. The shooting is close-at-hand and exciting.

Acquiring a Waterfowling Boat

Of course, the most common method of acquiring a waterfowling boat, is to simply buy one. And there are numerous boats on the market to satisfy almost any waterfowler's needs. Or you can simply rig your fishing boat to serve as a waterfowling boat.

However, many waterfowlers like the tradition of building their own rigs. There are numerous plans, as well as some kits on the market for constructing waterfowling boats.

7

Decoys:
From Reeds To Polyurethane

U sing decoys to lure wary waterfowl has always been a tradition with waterfowlers. Native Americans used mud clumps or "false" birds shaped of reeds. The market hunters of the 1800's used several hundred hand-carved wooden decoys for their deadly spreads. Decoys are just as important to today's waterfowlers. Heavily hunted, extra-wary waterfowl and the high competition from other hunters in some areas demands the best in decoys and their proper use.

Simply tossing out a handful of decoys won't guarantee success. You must match the decoys to the hunting situation whether it is field shooting, flooded timber, potholes, river sets or open water. The right type, size and numbers of decoys as well as the right spread pattern must be used for each situation.

Decoy Types

Decoys can and have been made of almost anything. There are decoys made of wood, cork, plastic, rubber and even old tires and empty soda pop bottles! There is also a wide variety of decoy designs each meant for a specific purpose. These include: *silhouette field decoys, full-bodied field decoys, full-bodied floater decoys,* and *inflatable decoys.*

The most commonly used decoys today are the plastic shell decoys. They are available from a number of different companies, in a

Decoys with weighted keels are self-righting in the water. That's an advantage when you're in a hurry and just want to throw the decoys into place.

complete line of duck, goose and confidence decoy species. One of the problems in selecting decoys may be the large variety of species available, as well as the different types of each species. Each type and species of decoy, however, will do a specific job better than others.

Floating Decoys

Plastics. The most popular type of decoy is a floater in standard size. These are also available in a variety of types including weighted- or nonweighted-keel.

The weighted-keel is the most popular, and with good reason. The weighted-keel utilizes a keel filled with ballast material; sand, lead, etc. When you toss these decoys into the water from the boat or shore, they automatically roll over and right themselves, regardless of how they land. Nonweighted-keel decoys don't always do that. And when setting out a spread in the dark, you may not notice a topsy-turvey decoy until it flares the first flock or two after shooting light!

There are hollow keel decoys which fill with water when the decoys are tossed into water. They are used primarily when weight is a problem, such as carrying a large number of decoys into a backwater slough or pothole. You must, however, place them carefully rather

Cabela's new "Bullet Proof" decoys can take a full charge of shot and show little effect.

than simply tossing them out because they will not always self-right.

One problem that has plagued hollow plastic decoy owners for years is decoys being shot while hunters finish at cripples on the water. The result is a decoy that takes on water, sits unnaturally or may even sink. The new Bullet-Proof Decoys from Cabela's are the answer to the problem. They are hollow plastic decoys that have been filled with closed-cell polyurethane foam. They can take a full load of Number 4 shot and still float.

I decided to test the decoys, as well as provide a dramatic photo, so I shot one at close range. To my amazement, the shot barely penetrated the outside shell, with many of the pellets evident from the outside. In addition the decoys, are high quality, and have a weighted keel running full length.

Another problem with purchased shell decoys is that all the heads are molded to face forward. This doesn't make a very realistic set. John Gleason, a fellow waterfowler and outdoor writer cuts the heads off with a hacksaw, then glues them back on at different angles and facing different directions.

But Outdoorsman International of Beaver Dam, Wisconsin provides an alternate, store-bought solution. They produce a paper-mache type decoy with moveable heads. These are the old Herter's model that some veteran waterfowlers have used for years.

Cork. There are also several cork decoys being manufactured. For the most part they are duck decoys, but there are also some cork goose floaters being made. These are all big, heavy-weight decoys, and are extremely durable. Some of them come with wooden heads, others with plastic heads. Some of the better ones have heads that can be turned on the bodies. This provides a chance to vary the decoy set, with some heads turned different directions.

Cork decoys do have several advantages over hollow plastic shell decoys. The biggest is that they sit heavier and more naturally in the water. They aren't bothered by heavy winds or waves, which often cause shell decoys to flop about. They can also take an occasional shot load without being damaged too much. Another advantage is that their finish stays dull, regardless of how wet they get. Many plastic shell decoys take on a shine once they become wet, or when they are constantly exposed to heavy waves.

There are a couple of disadvantages to cork decoys, probably the biggest is weight. They are heavy and bulky. They are also quite a bit higher in cost than plastic shell decoys.

Wood. There are still a few wooden decoy manufacturers. Wooden decoys have many of the same advantages as cork over the

In selecting decoys, pay special attention to the species you're likely to encounter in your hunting areas. Here the author puts out some tiny teal blocks.

plastic shell decoys. They do, however, often weigh a great deal more, and they are extremely expensive.

Rubber. Another type of duck "floater" decoy is the inflatable rubber decoy. These are light-weight, (about eight ounces each), and are easy to carry. You can fit a dozen in your hunting coat quite easily. They are ideal for that pothole or slough a couple miles from the road. To use, you merely toss into the air. They're open on the bottom and air is caught inside, inflating them as they fall. About their only disadvantage is they are not quite as realistic as many of the other decoys.

Decoys To Create Movement

There are also decoys that create "movement." They include several different styles of animated decoys. Available are swimming decoys that glide back and forth tethered to a line tied between two stakes. There is also a "fluttering" type of decoy that rocks vigorously and adds ripples to the set. There is also a "feeding" decoy with only the tail protruding which also flutters to simulate a feeding puddle duck.

Although I got a lot of kidding from fellow hunters when I tested these decoys, the results caused many scoffers to order their own motorized decoys. They are available in several different species and sizes. Another use I found for the moving decoys was to keep ice from freezing back in holes I opened in pothole hunting late in the season. The movement of the decoys kept a good 12-foot-wide hole open for several hours, and provided some extremely good late- season shooting.

There are also "flying" decoys which utilize kites or wind socks to simulate the movement of flying or landing ducks or geese. Made in the shape of a wind sock, they are available in both mallard and all goose species. They can be positioned on poles over either a water or field set and simulate flying birds coming into the decoys. They are extremely lightweight and easy to carry. You can easily pack a good number of these decoys out to a goose field. The only problem I found is they don't provide a very convincing appearance on days without wind, nor in rain or ice. But on blustery, windy, days they can really add realism to your spread.

Field Decoys

Full-bodies. There is also a variety of field decoys available. The most popular, again, is the plastic hollow-shell body. They sit on wooden stakes pushed into the ground. There are also full-bodied

Motorized or mechanical decoys add lifelike motion to your set and help keep the ice at bay on cold mornings.

field decoys of hollow plastic bodies. They come in several species, including Canada, snow, blue and white-fronted goose. Since most of the field hunting is for geese, the majority of the field decoys are for geese. There are, however, some for mallards and pintails.

Because it takes a large number of field decoys to entice a flock of geese, one important factor in selecting this type of decoy is the ease of carrying. Portability and weight as well as how they assemble and are set up are important factors.

As with all decoy spreads, the single most important factor in selecting decoys is to match the decoy species to the species you're hunting.

Although Canadas will occasionally come into snow decoys, rarely will snows and blues come into primarily a Canada set. The spread, however, can be set with enough of both to entice the different species.

Silhouettes. At one time there was a big interest in silhouette field decoys for geese. These became popular because the shell bodied geese of the past were not particularly long lasting. Silhouette geese made of thin plywood or plastic quickly became a favorite. With the nesting, easy-to-carry lightweight and long lasting shell bodies produced today, there is little use for silhouette goose decoys. They are still popular with hunters who prefer to make their own.

Rags. Though they are among the simplest of all decoys, diapers

The shell decoy, whether store-bought or home-made, is the standard for many field goose hunters.

or "rags" are very effective, especially on light goose species. Just about anything with a white finish has been tried and worked, including diapers, paper table clothes, bleach bottles and paper plates. However, each of these materials has its own drawbacks. Diapers get unbearably heavy when wet. "Banquet cloth" can only be used once or twice before it falls apart. Bleach bottles are bulky. And paper plates are really too small and tend to blow away.

The solution is in the form of square sheets of plastic printed with goose markings. They're called "Sheet Decs" and produced by Texas Hunting Products out of Houston.

Sheet Decs are available in a number of patterns including snow goose, blue goose, immature snow goose, and Canada goose. These rags have proven effective from Manitoba to Texas. They're nonreflective and can be used year after year. They are especially effective used in large numbers and mixed with full-body decoys.

Decoy Size

The size of the decoys you choose is very important. In early season hunting, small pothole, pond, flooded timber or slough hunting, standard size decoys are usually the choice. For late season, wary waterfowl and hunting open waters of lakes and bays, howev-

When it comes to field goose hunting, numbers play an important part in decoying success. Note that these hunters have wisely separated the species within their spread.

er, the best choice would be the magnum, super magnum or even larger decoys. The size and weight of the larger decoys does have some disadvantages. To give you an idea of the size difference, most standard mallard decoys are approximately 15 to 16 inches long. The magnums are usually 18 to 20 inches long while the super magnums may be as big as 23 to 24 inches.

Species

Decoys are made to match most species. Again, the most productive method of hunting is to match the decoy to the species being hunted. Some duck species, however, will decoy to other species. For instance, wood ducks and wigeons will come quite readily into almost any decoys.

Early, during the teal season, many waterfowlers like to use the tiny blocks to draw in the early birds, though teal will also decoy to almost any type of dabbler decoy, such as mallards. Other early season species may also be mixed in with a mallard set early in the season. As the season progresses these early migrators should be removed from the set.

In decoying geese, it's also important to recognize which species you're likely to en-counter in your hunting area and plan accordingly.

In areas where there are both dabbler and diving ducks as well as geese, all three should be used in the set. The decoys, however, should not be intermixed, but should be grouped by individual species. Although the stools can be placed side by side, there should be separate landing pockets for each species.

When setting out a stool of several species, remember that diving ducks usually land at the head of the rig while puddle ducks normally land at the back of the rig. Dabblers usually won't fly over any decoys and geese also rarely fly over decoys, so your spread should be rigged accordingly. Most gunners feel that rigs should have about the same number of hens and drakes to be effective.

A good set for the middle to late part of the season would consist of a primary set of mallards with a small group of pintails set off to one side and grouped tightly together. There should also be a primary set of scaup, again, set off to one side, but almost joining the mallard group. Then a set of Canada or snow geese acting as "confidence" decoys could be added.

One problem today is that many hunters set out only one or two Canada decoys for a duck set. To make the set more effective, a dozen or more Canadas should be used. This is particuarly true on open reservoirs and lakes that get quite a bit of hunting pressure. If hunting from the shoreline, you should also have a good number of feeding goose field decoys in your spread.

The primary species will, of course, change with the predominance of certain species of waterfowl across the country. For instance, in areas frequented mostly by pintails, you may prefer a primary pintail set, while an area that has mostly canvasbacks will, of course, need a predominantly canvasback set.

Confidence Decoys

Many waterfowlers also like to use confidence decoys, or those birds that are typically so wary that by their very presence they signal a safe haven to other birds. Goose decoys placed with a duck spread can act as confidence decoys, however, there are also a number of specialty confidence decoys that can be used. Probably the ultimate confidence decoy for shallow water is a great blue heron. This wary bird should be placed about 100 yards from your decoy spread. In addition, there are other shore confidence decoys including, golden plovers, egrets, crows, etc.

Open water confidence decoys include coots and seagulls. These are often used in conjunction with layout, sculling or sneak rigs or simply near an open water blind to encourage incoming birds.

Simple coot blocks are among the most effective confidence decoys.

Numbers Of Decoys

Once you decide what type and species of decoy to use, the next question is, how many? In most instances, the answer is as many as you can afford and can transport. There are, however, situations when only a handful of decoys can be very productive.

Areas that have small flocks will normally require smaller numbers of decoys. On the other hand, when large groups of feeding or resting birds are in the same area, you will need the appropriate number of decoys. Remember, that in most instances large numbers of birds mean safety to other birds. For the most part, the larger spreads are the most effective. The exception is if you're gunning small sheltered waters or hunting green timber. In the latter just a half-dozen decoys is the norm and is all you need to be effective.

By the same token, an area that gets little hunting needs only a few decoys. A heavily hunted area that has quite a bit of competition among hunters needs large numbers of decoys to compete with nearby hunters. This is especially true when it comes to field hunting for geese. The larger spread will nearly always out-pull a smaller rig, all other conditions being the same.

Rigging

There is almost as much variation in decoy rigging as there is in decoy choice. Again, the most important rule is to suit the rigging to the hunting situation. This depends mostly on how many decoys are needed, as well as the water depth. Shallow water sets are not particularly hard to handle. Just make sure you have enough line to proper-

Plan the rigging for your deep water decoy spread carefully, or you're likely to en-counter a time-wasting mess.

ly set the decoys. Use only good quality nylon decoy anchor cord
which is available in dark brown or green. Unless you hunt in the ex-
act same spot all the time and the water depth stays exactly the same,
it's a good idea to keep a little excess decoy line on the keel. This can
be held in place either with a rubber band, or with a half-hitch around
the end of the keel.

The biggest frustration with decoys is the tangles that can occur.
Waterfowlers have fought the problem for years, but the solution is
really quite simple. When making a shallow water set with individual anchors on each decoy, use the soft lead wrap-around anchors. It
makes setting out and picking up decoys a much easier chore. With
the anchor and cord firmly wrapped around the neck of the decoy,
the problem of loose and tangled cords is solved. In heavy seas,
however, the lightweight, bendable anchors may pull loose. The
best anchors for heavy weather are the larger mushroom shaped anchors that will dig into the bottom and hold.

Decoy rigging for large open water sets often require a bit more
work. The first requirement, of course, is longer lines. You will also
need heavier anchors to hold the long line, and decoys in place in
rough water. Because large numbers of decoys are required, as well
as the tangles caused by single rigged decoys at greater depths, sets
for open water are quite often made with a single line. Individual decoys are fastened to the line with rings and clips. This is a set- up
quite like a fishing trotline. In this case the anchor weights and the
main line must be quite a bit heavier. Old-time window sash weights
or bricks are the best choice for weights in this situation. Parachute
cording is often the choice for the main line. An excellent source for
multiple decoy rigs is *Decoy Rigs, P.O. Box 366, Whiting, Indiana
46394.*

One of the biggest hassles of decoys is carrying them. If traveling by boat, decoys are usually tossed in piles in the boat. When
hunting backwater sloughs or potholes, however, decoys must be
carried in on your back. The best method is to use one of the nylon
mesh sacks to store and carry decoys. Other sacks can be used, but
will often become a heavy, frozen mess when trying to carry out wet
decoys. It helps to store decoys in these sacks even when transport-
ing them by boat. You can sort them according to species, etc. thus
making setting and retrieving decoys much easier.

When purchasing a decoy sack consider the various sizes and
quality levels. Nothing is more frustrating than having the bottom
bust out of a decoy bag when you face a half mile hike through a
mucky, muddy field.

For shallow water, the rigging need consist only of a cord and anchor. You can neat-ly store the line by wrapping it around the head or keel of the decoy.

Setting The Spread

Although there are numerous different individual ways of setting out decoys, there are just three basic decoying situations: 1)*a shoreline blind, which may be a river, lake, pothole or slough; 2)an open water blind* on a large lake or bay; and 3)*field shooting* for ducks or geese.

There are also a good number of different patterns, including the traditional J-hook and its variations, which I believe is the most commonly used.

Regardless of which situation or pattern, there is one important rule that you must always remember in setting out your spread. *Waterfowl always land into the wind!*

Keep this in mind and you can not only make your spread look correct to entice waterfowl, but you can also set the spread for the most effective gunning opportunities as well.

Again, the decoys must be properly grouped according to species and positioned so an open landing pocket for each species will not only be within easy shotgun reach, but also provide you with shots to your best advantage. For instance, if you are a right-handed shooter, the best passing shots are usually from your right hand side to your left. By positioning the decoy pocket to your left you will make the birds swing more that way and vice versa. Shown in the illustrations are a number of different sets according to wind direction, etc.

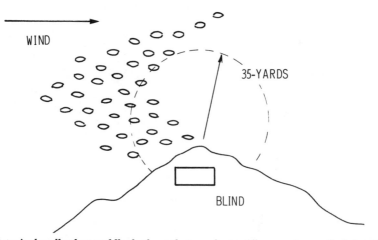

A typical mallard or puddle duck set that can be used for marsh or pothole hunting. Puddle ducks normally do not like to fly over land or decoys. Note open landing pocket in front of blind.

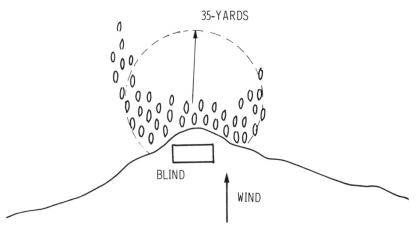

This set can be adapted for wind direction. This is one of the easiest decoying sets.

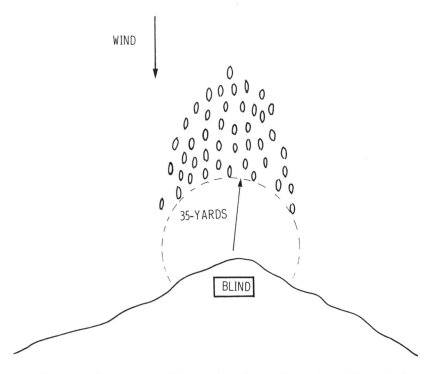

Anything is worth a try, but you'll have a hard time pulling in the puddlers with this spread. To land they have to swing in over the land area.

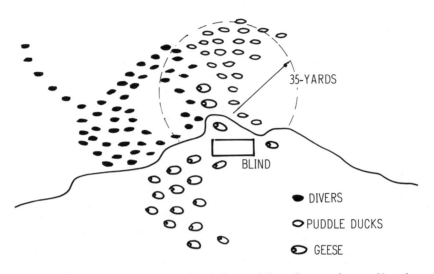

This is a typical multi-species spread including puddlers, divers and geese. Note the three distinct landing pockets.

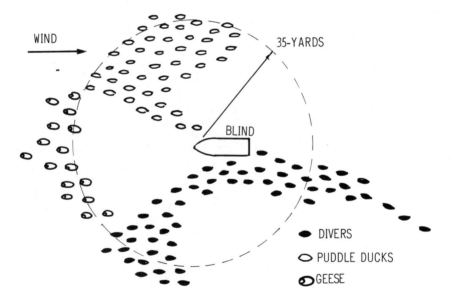

A typical open water multi-species set again offers three separate landing pockets. Note the long leading line to attract divers.

Making Your Own Decoys

You can also make your own decoys quite easily. Some space to work and only a few tools are necessary. Handmade decoys can be the easy-to-make goose silhouettes, or handcarved cork or wooden decoys.

Silhouettes. Cutting goose silhouettes from 1/4-inch marine plywood is an easy chore that requires only a space to work plus a saber saw. Make a pattern from heavy cardboard, then transfer this to the plywood. Cut out the outline, with a saber saw, sand the edges smooth, then install a stake on the bottom with screws. Paint the decoys with a good decoy paint or *flat* latex house paint.

Cork Full-bodied Decoys. The next easier method of building decoys is to utilize cork for full bodied decoys. It's much easier to shape and carve than wood. You will, however, have to glue a wooden head and wooden bottom and keel in place as shown in the illustrations.

First step is to enlarge the squared drawing to make a full- sized pattern. Then glue the plywood bottom on the cork blocks. Cut this

1" SQUARES

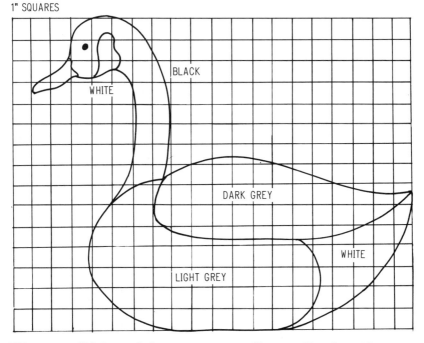

This pattern will help you design your own goose silhouettes. Note that each square represents one square inch.

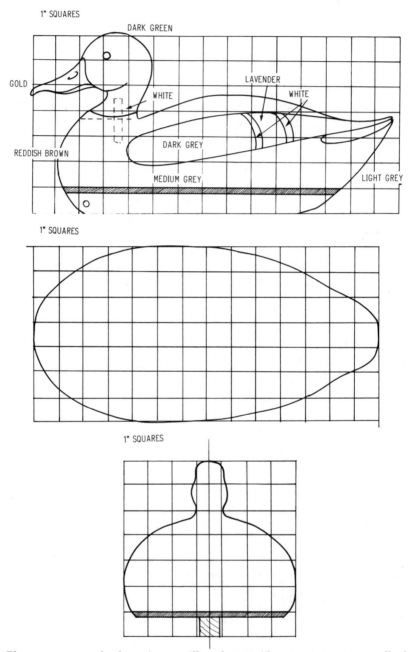

These patterns are the three views you'll need to consider to carve your own mallard decoys. Note that each square represents one square inch.

1" SQUARES

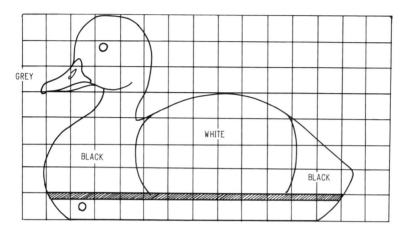

This pattern shows the relative size and coloration of a diving duck decoy. Note that each square represents one square inch.

to rough shape with a bandsaw then finish with an open cut wood rasp. Shape the head in the same manner, then fasten in place in the cork body with a dowel and waterproof glue. Paint to suit.

Wood Full-bodied Decoys. You can also make your own wood decoys, but it takes more effort in carving. To lighten the weight the decoys should be made in three sections so you can create a hollow body as shown in the illustrations. Rough out the glued block on a bandsaw, then final shape with a rasp and sander. Hand sand and then paint to suit.

No matter which route you go, building requires some effort and with the price of materials today, you probably won't be saving much money in the process. But the pay off is the deep felt satisfaction of taking ducks or geese over blocks that you made yourself!

A great deal of practice and knowledge of waterfowl is brought together in the sweet notes of duck music produced by a champion caller like Bill Harper.

8

Calling Waterfowl

One of the most important yet least understood facets of waterfowl hunting is calling. Good calling is extremely important to waterfowl success. Bad calling is worse than no calling at all!

Proper calling is not a hard-to-learn, mysterious process. It is a fun skill that almost anyone can learn to do.

There are many different techniques used for the various waterfowl species. These include calls for puddle ducks, diver ducks, "whistling ducks" such as teal and wood ducks, plus the various goose calls.

There are, of course, a number of different calls that can be used to produce this variety of sounds. In fact, there are so many different types of calls on the market today it may seem quite confusing at first glance. Although all calls of a certain kind, for instance, the common duck call, are made to produce approximately the same sound, there is a wide variation in their tone, ease of blowing, durability, appearance, etc.

Choosing A Call

Selecting a waterfowling call is a very personal thing. What works for some might not for others. This can only be done by trial and error, to determine the call that suits the individual hunter. Most good sporting emporiums have a selection of demonstrator calls that you can try. A knowledgeable clerk can offer good advice, but try

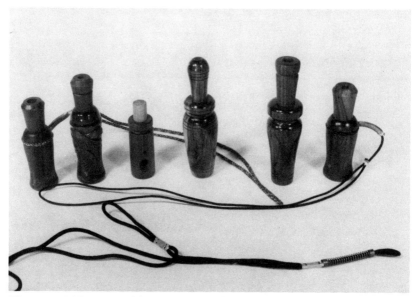

There are a wide variety of duck and goose calls on the market. Choosing the one that will work best for you is a matter of trying them out.

out every one they have available to see which you like best.

Types of Calls

Waterfowl calls are made of a variety of materials including hardwoods, several different kinds of plastic, as well as rubber. There are, however, just four basic types of waterfowl calls.

The first is the standard duck call, which can be made of wood or plastic, and produces a variety of different quacking sounds made by most puddle ducks, particularly mallards.

The second is the diver call which produces the *"brrrrrrr"* buzzing sound of diver ducks.

The third is the whistle call that produces the sounds of teal, wood ducks, pintail and widgeon.

The fourth group consists of several types of goose calls which produce the shrill honks, laughs and shrieks of various goose species. These are broken into several categories which we'll discuss in a moment.

There is a variety of each of these calls made by the numerous manufacturers. All of the quality, brand-name calls will work. Again, it's more a matter of finding a call that works the best for you!

Be Prepared

Regardless of what type and brand of call is chosen, it's a good idea to have several calls on hand. Even the best ones can become clogged or waterlogged at the wrong moment. It is also a good idea to keep the calls on a lanyard so they can't accidentally be dropped or lost.

Learning To Call

There are several methods of learning to call waterfowl. The best is to simply spend time in a blind with an expert waterfowl caller who will take the time to teach you proper calling techniques.

There is no better substitute than being in a hunting situation, hearing the various calls, and watching the reactions of waterfowl.

The next best bet is to listen to one of the waterfowl calling tapes produced by the numerous call manufacturers. These tapes illustrate the best methods for each particular call. They also teach how to produce the variety of sounds that are used to call waterfowl.

Then it's merely a matter of practice, practice and more practice. Incidentally, more than one duck hunter has learned to call while driving back and forth to work.

Another thing that can help better your calling is to spend time in the marshes or waterfowl habitat, listening to and calling to birds in the wild. Observe how they react to the call and to each other's sounds. This doesn't have to be during the hunting season, in fact, during the spring when birds are migrating north is a good time to observe them and learn to call. And most likely you'll have the marsh and the birds all to yourself.

Calling Puddle Ducks

The most commonly used call is the quack sound used by mallards and other puddle ducks. In fact, almost all duck species will respond to the calls made by mallards.

The call most commonly used is a tube type made of wood or plastic. There is a shaker type call that can be used to make some of the sounds, however, the tube call that is blown by mouth is by far the most popular.

The first step in learning to properly blow the call is learning how to hold it. Grasp the end of the call by encircling it with your thumb and forefinger. Then cup your fingers to form a sort of ''bell'' around the end of the call. This provides you with the opportunity to control the sound by opening and closing your fingers.

Place the call on the inside of the bottom lip, then bring it up

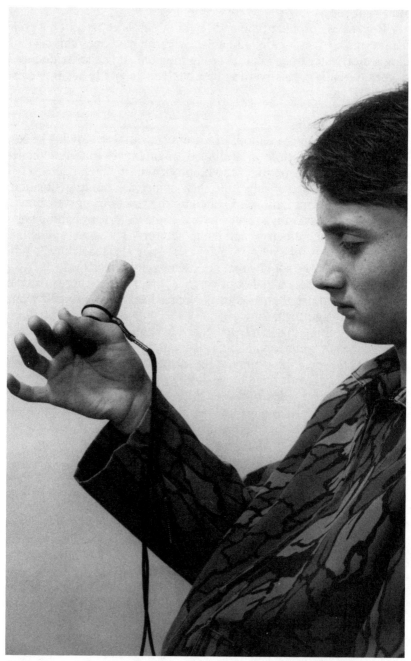

The proper technique is to grip the call between the thumb and index finger.

The call should be placed on the bottom lip and positioned against the upper lip.

Do not puff out your cheeks when blowing a duck call! The air should come from the diaphragm, creating a grunting sound.

For experienced callers, pushing air from the chest is second nature.

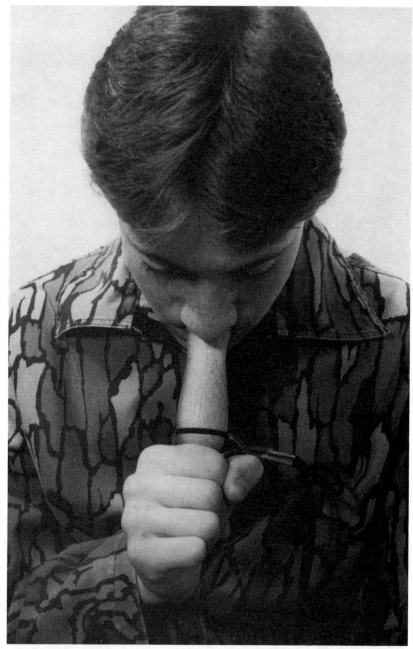

The tone of the call can be varied by opening and closing the hand or holding the call against the chest.

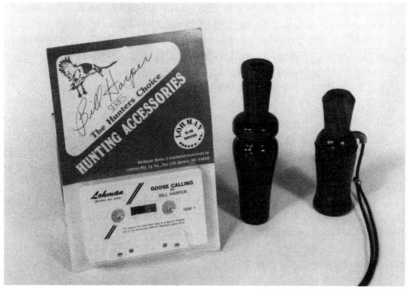

For most hunters, the best learning tool is a high quality instructional cassette tape. Videos are also very popular.

against the outside of your upper lip. With the call in place, close your lips tightly. Make sure no air can escape except through the call.

The call is not blown with air from the mouth. Instead air is brought up from the chest, rolling the diaphragm upward to force a large volume of air through the call. When done correctly, this will produce a "grunt" that is audible along with the sounds made through the call. Without this force of air into the throat and through the call, the sounds made will be hollow and high pitched.

At the same time you force air through the call you must say a "word-sound." There are a number of different word sounds that can be used.

Bill Harper, President of Lohman Game Call Company and expert caller in his own right, uses three words to teach callers to use his calls. They are *"wick," "tick-it,"* and *"kak."*

Granted, it will take some time to learn to say the words and produce the correct amount of air pressure through the call to produce proper sounds. It's much like riding a bicycle or learning other skills. At first it will seem quite awkward, but with practice can easily be learned. Finally, when real ducks are on the wing, it will be second nature.

"Wick". The word *wick* is used to produce the quacking sounds of a hen mallard. Start by saying the word *wick* and blowing through the call. By stretching the word out and changing the tone by moving your fingers you can make a variety of different sounding "quacks." Once you learn to make the basic quack sound, the next step is to learn to string together at least five of the quacks.

"Tick-it". The second basic sound, *tick-it*, is used to produce the feeding chuckles made by puddle ducks. Say the word *tick-it* into the call, fluttering your tongue at the same time you force air through the call. Start slowly, and continue practicing until you can continuously say the word fast enough to produce a sort of soft, chuckling sound.

This is extremely awkward to learn at first. It's akin to the tongue twisters you tried as a kid. But if you start slowly and work up to speed, it can be learned quite easily.

"Kak". The third basic sound is the word *kak* which is used to produce the clucking sound of a hen mallard. This can be mixed in with the feeding chatter to produce a realistic series of calls. To produce the sound say the word *kak* into the call, again as you grunt from the chest. This is a fairly easy call to learn.

Putting It All Together

Once you have mastered the basic sounds made with the call, the next step is to learn to produce a variety of different calling patterns that can be used for various hunting situations.

There are six basic calling patterns including the hail or highball call, the close-in hail call, the comeback call, close-in confidence call, lonesome hen call, and the feeding call.

The Hail or Highball. This call is used to attract the attention of distant ducks. It's loud, demanding and can be used to call ducks as far away as a half mile or more. It should not, however, be used when ducks are close in, or less than 200 yards. The call is made by saying the word *wick* into the call as loud as possible. Force air into the call until the sound "breaks" on a high note. Hold the high, loud sound for the count of five. Once you learn to do this, practice making the loud, high pitched call five times in a row, then come down the scale in volume and pitch as fast as possible.

The Close-in Hail Call. This is a softer, shorter version of the hail call. It is also called the "five quack," "landing," or as duck hunting friend Dell Arduzer says, the "sit-down" call. It consists of five fairly short, fast quacks. It starts high and comes down the scale, in volume and tone. Some hunters, like Dell, stretch out the first quack. This call is especially effective when ducks are warily circling the blind, about 50 to 100 yards away. It can often be mixed with the feed call for a very effective combination.

The close-in call can also be used when ducks are warily circling your decoys. It is a sort of stretched out begging sound made by pronouncing the word *wi———-ck* in a long, stretched-out sound. The pattern starts fairly high and comes down the scale fairly slow, and low. It should be given four or five times and mixed in with feeding calls for the best results.

The Comeback Call. It starts fairly high like the hail call, but not as loud. The word *wick* is used three times, coming down the scale extremely fast. The word *wick* is then said three or four more times, getting slower towards the end. The last sounds should be sort of stretched-out and begging. It is especially effective when ducks start to land just outside your decoys.

The Lonesome Hen Call. Often given with the feed chatter to entice cautious ducks, it can also be extremely effective on single drakes or small flocks of waterfowl. It is a series of soft calls using the word *wick* to produce raspy, soft quacks, and the word *kak* to produce the cluck. This is mixed in with the feed chatter.

The last part of the pattern consists of long, drawn-out pleading quacks using the word *wick*.

Whistle Calls

Teal, pintail, widgeon and wood ducks can be called with the quacks and patterns given for mallards. It also helps to sometimes add in the special whistling sounds these species make to provide an even more realistic calling pattern. This can be done using nothing more than a toy police whistle, however, there are numerous specialty calls on the market for making these whistling sounds.

These whistle calls are usually blown fairly softly to produce the soft twitterings and whistles of these different duck species. For effect the calls should be mixed in with soft quacks as well. It helps to have two callers in the blind, one providing the whistling sounds and another the quacks.

Calling Diving Ducks

Diving ducks will also respond quite readily to the puddle duck calls, however, they also produce their own sounds that are somewhat different. Again, adding these sounds to the calling pattern can make it more realistic and often convince otherwise wary divers to come on in.

There are a number of whistle calls available. This model produces the call of a number of whistling waterfowl species.

There are a number of different calls manufactured to produce the sounds of diving ducks. These sounds for the most part are sharp, bark-like calls, deep growls and *"purrrrrrrs"* mixed in with soft quacks. You can produce these calls to some degree on a common mallard call by fluttering your tongue against the roof of your mouth and grunting into your duck call at the same time. However, a call especially made for producing the diver sounds makes the sounds much easier and more realistic.

One thing to remember is that most diving ducks call very fast. When you see a group of divers, start giving a series of very high, fast quacks. As the birds get closer start lowering the pitch of the quacks and adding in the purrs and growls.

Learning To Call Geese

Although calling geese is similar in many ways to calling ducks, there are several differences. For the most part goose calls are a bit larger and are easier to blow. They are held and positioned against the lips in much the same manner as duck calls. In most instances, however, goose calls are simply blown through, rather than using the grunt as is done with duck calls. Some callers prefer to use the grunting technique.

Like duck calls, there are a number of different calls manufactured for the various goose species. Canada goose calls are the most common and they can also be used to call the other goose species. The sounds for other species such as snows, blues and specklebellies, however, are much higher pitched, sharper and quicker and a lot more demanding. For this reason, savvy hunters who hunt several goose species prefer to carry separate calls for the different species.

Calling Canada Geese

Just as in calling ducks, the best method of calling Canadas is to say a word into the call at the same time you blow air through it.

The words used to call Canada geese are *"what,"* *"hut,"* and *"ha-ha-ha-ha-ha."* Using these three words you can produce all the sounds needed to call Canadas.

What. The honking sound of geese is made by saying the word *"what"* into the call, breaking it up into two syllables. The sound should start low with a *whaaaa-* and end up with a sharp, higher pitched *t* sound on the end. Breath pressure should be fairly low on the first part of the two-syllable call, building up slowly until the sound breaks up to the higher pitched sound caused when more air is forced through the call. The final sharp end of the sound is made as the tongue contacts the roof of the mouth immediately behind the front teeth.

Start learning the call slowly until you can give a nice even two note call. The biggest problem is learning how to produce the correct amount of air pressure to get the sounds. It takes a good deal of air pressure on some calls to achieve the higher pitched sound. This will take some experimentation. Once you have learned to make the individual call, then learn to do it four or five times without taking a breath or removing the call from your mouth.

"Hut." The next sound is the word *"hut."* This word said through the call produces the very short feeding honk or cluck that Canada geese use while feeding. It's also a very good landing call.

"Ha-Ha-Ha-Ha-Ha." The last word is *"ha-ha-ha-ha-ha."* This is the gabble or feeding chatter made by feeding geese. By saying the word and at the same time huffing short puffs of air through the call, you produce the low note of the two-note goose call. Try the sound very slowly until you master it, then begin saying it in a very fast series to simulate feeding chatter.

Putting It Together For Canada Geese

Just as with duck calling, these sounds must be made in a series or pattern to lure geese to your decoys. The first call is a greeting call and is used when you spot geese some distance from your blind. First, however, make a note of the flight pattern of the geese. If they are in a distinct line or a ''V,'' they are flight geese and probably won't respond to the call. If on the other hand, they are in small flocks or family groups, they will probably come to the call. One exception to this is when you're dealing with huge flocks of birds in the early stages of the migration. There are many young birds in these groups, and they can often be lured away from the flock despite what their elders might be telling them.

Give several of the *"what"* two note honks, until the flock starts to turn toward your decoys. As the geese approach your spread, increase the speed of your calling, becoming more ''desperate'' sounding with the call. Some callers like to add a couple more high notes to the call each time, before dropping back down to the low note making it sound like several geese are calling.

Once it becomes evident the geese are coming in, start adding in the feeding and gabble calls. Mix these in with a few well spaced honks. Once the geese set their wings and start to come in over the decoys, stop calling completely. This is where most geese are lost to over-anxious callers.

By opening and closing your hand over the end of the call, you can produce more varied sounds with your calls. Goose calling is one of those situations where you almost can't get too many callers. The more racket and noise, the more realistic it will sound to geese. When you have a couple hundred big honkers hovering over the top of you continuously "kerhonking" to each other you will be amazed at the racket they make.

Bleat Calling

There is another type of Canada goose calling used on the Midwest grain fields as well as the Eastern Coast. It's called bleat calling, and there are special calls to make the sound, however, you can easily make it using a standard goose call. The sound consists of a series of standard honks. It is actually nothing more than continuous honking until you have geese heading toward the decoys with wings locked up. The caller then changes to a very fast feed call using nothing but the word "*hut.*" This will get the geese very excited and they will often decoy very fast. Harold Knight of Knight & Hale Game Calls has an excellent tape on this tactic of calling geese.

Calling Snow and Blue Geese

Snow and blue geese are very vocal when in flight or feeding, and their high pitched calls sound more like a small barking dog. The three words used for calling snow geese are: "*what,*" "*ha-ha-ha-ha-ha,*" and "*tut.*"

The first two sounds are made as in calling Canada geese. The pattern, however, is faster and higher pitched using a snow and blue goose call. The last word, *tut* is also used to make the single note honk or feed honk made when incoming snows are landing in a flock.

The pattern for calling snows and blues is also similar to Canadas and consists of a series of two-note honks until the geese start to swing in closer. Then the tempo is increased and the "*tut-tut-tut-tut*" sounds are added in along with the feeding chatter. When the geese set their wings, give a feed call and gabble mixed with well spaced, single loud honks that signify the all's clear signal.

Calling Specklebellies

The call made by specklebellies is a very high pitched cackling sound almost like someone laughing. This gives them the nickname cackling or laughing geese. The words used to call specklebellies are

"wha," "ha-ha-ha" as used in the feeding gabble, and *"ku-luck."*
When in flight, the *"wah-wah-wah-wah-wah"* sound is made. The feeding sound is made with *"ha-ha-ha-ha."* The short grunt or honk sound is a high pitched *"ku-luck"* that should be added interspersed through the feeding chatter.

No Calling

Again, for all waterfowl calling the best advice is, ''No calling is better than bad calling!'' This especially true in goose hunting. Many times the birds will swing into a spread of well-placed decoys without a single note blown on the call. And when you have huge flocks swirling around your set, *don't call!* In the din and confusion they probably won't hear a single call anyway! Now's the time to go ahead and concentrate on your shooting and the moment!

9

Dogs For The Waterfowl Hunter

A good retriever can enhance the hunt, and make a day of water-fowling a joy. A poor retriever can make the day a most frustrating experience. Hunting without a dog can send you home sickened by the thought of the cripples you could have collected had you shared the day with a canine companion.

Pure and simple, a well-trained retriever is the single most important conservation measure a waterfowler can take. No matter how good a shot you are, you are going to occasionally cripple a bird or have one fall in heavy cover. And no matter how good you think you are at marking falls, you're going to lose some birds without a dog to get to the bird fast!

To be sure, even the best dog is going to miss a bird occasionally, but not nearly as many as you will unaided by a sensitive canine nose!

Some waterfowl hunters take it to the extreme and suggest that if you don't have a dog, you shouldn't hunt ducks. Period!

Now that's a little extreme because of the wide variation in the types of hunting situations we have available to us in North America. But if you choose or are forced to hunt without a dog, *pick your shots carefully!* Never slap the trigger on a duck or goose that has the slightest possibility of falling where you can't see it! And make sure it's dead! There's nothing unsporting about doing whatever is necessary to finish off and retrieve a downed bird.

Good Dogs, Bad Dogs

There are numerous breeds of dogs that make excellent retrievers, and many dogs that are not full-blooded retrievers can also be excellent blind companions and staunch bird locators. Regardless of the breed, the most important factor in the difference between a good retriever and a poor one, is obedience. If the dog is of good blood, retrieving will come easy. However if the dog won't mind, he will not only ruin many hunts, but can be dangerous to hunters as well.

Choosing Your Retriever

The first step is to choose the breed. There are numerous retriever breeds from which to choose. You should consider your particular hunting situations, as well as other considerations you might have concerning living year round with the dog. Some breeds are more suited for certain situations than others.

For instance Chesepeake Bay Retrievers, or "chessies" are one of the hardiest breeds, but are often not easy-going house pets. On the other hand, Golden Retrievers make excellent house pets, as well as waterfowl retrievers, but they are not quite as hardy under extremely cold weather conditions.

Labrador Retriever. Probably the most popular of retrievers, the Labrador is a smooth, straight-coated, solidly-built dog. They are most commonly black, but are often found in yellow and chocolate variations. They normally weigh from 65 to 70 pounds. They are very intelligent and easily trained. They are also extremely friendly and make good pets, as well as hunting companions. Labs usually get along with other dogs quite well and can be used in extreme weather conditions for both water or field work.

They can also be taught to hunt upland game in the flushing manner, making them a good double-duty dog for those who also enjoy hunting upland game.

Chesepeake Bay Retriever. The most aggressive and hardest working of all the retrievers, the Chessie is also the hardiest. They have a heavy, oily, curly coat that protects them in even the iciest water and foulest weather. They are larger than most retrievers, often weighing over 90 pounds. For the serious waterfowl hunter who doesn't want a house pet, they are tops. They will quite often fight with other dogs, however. Their aggressive temperament also makes them a bit harder to train than other retrievers. Their color is a dead grass to dark brown that blends well in the blind or boat. They are extremely aggressive retrievers which can only be appreciated by seeing them jump from blind or boat into icy water.

Labrador retrievers are the most popular dog with waterfowl hunters. Their willing-ness to please, gentle nature and intelligence are the reasons why.

Chesapeake Bay retrievers are excellent waterfowl retrieving specialists. They're at their best when conditions are at their worst.

Golden Retriever. Considered by many as the most beautiful and stylish of the retrievers, Goldens are not only fine water dogs, they make excellent pets as well. They have long, silky hair, which is usually a light gold, but may run to auburn. Their light coat is not as effective in extreme weather, but they are excellent retrievers in mild climates. They are considered the best for nonslip retrieving, and obedience.

Goldens are not as aggressive as many other retrievers, however, their friendliness and easy-to-train capabilities make them excellent gunning dogs for the one-dog hunter. They can also be trained to make excellent upland flushing dogs as well. Their long coats do cause some problems in keeping them clean of the burrs and debris they pick up during a day in the field.

Curly-Coated Retriever. Although not particularly popular in the United States, the Curly-Coated Retriever is a favorite elsewhere. Somewhat smaller and lighter than many other retrievers, they are extremely sturdy and aggressive, particularly in extremely cold weather. They are intelligent, easy-to-train dogs, and make excellent retrievers. About their only drawback is their heavy curly coat which needs quite a bit of care. It consists of tightly curled ringlets and is heavy. The tail of the retriever is usually carried straight back.

Irish Water Spaniel. Another less popular breed in America, the Irish Water Spaniel was bred to retrieve in the cold boggy marshes of Ireland. It has a thick, curly coat that protects it well in extreme weather conditions. However, that same coat takes a great deal of care. The breed is usually dark brown or black and has a ratlike tail. The tail also gives it the nickname Rat-Tailed Retriever. Larger than other spaniels, the Rat-Tailed Irishman weighs around 65 pounds. The Irish is usually considered a one-man dog and sometimes won't get along with other hunters or their dogs. They are somewhat hard headed and take a bit of expertise to train.

Flat-Coated Retriever. Also called the Wavy-Coated Retriever, this is also an excellent water dog. The breed, however, has never been very popular with American gunners. They are a solidly-built, muscular retriever with a flat heavy coat, that can withstand extremely rough weather. They are usually black or dark brown.

American Water Spaniel. A smaller breed, typical of the spaniels, they make an excellent all-purpose dog that can be used on upland game as well as for retrieving ducks and geese. The breed is just becoming popular again in the United States, because of their all-around uses and easy-going spaniel-like temperament.

Other Breeds. There are several other breeds that can double as both flushing or pointing upland dogs as well as retrievers for waterfowl. They are not, however, "waterfowling specialists" and usually don't do the job at hand quite as well as dogs bred specifically for handling rugged conditions and big, tough birds. They do, however, provide the one-dog hunter with a good all-around dog that can be used for anything that walks or flies the marshes, streams or upland fields.

A good example is the Springer Spaniel. These hardy little, hard-working dogs are excellent on both upland game and as retrievers. They make a great all-around dog with as pleasant a temperament as you could ask for. Their fine hair doesn't afford the cold water protection of the retriever breeds, but they'll turn in brilliant performances regardless.

By the same token the Weimaraner, although primarily known as an upland game dog, will also work quite well as a water dog in mild climates. Another breed that works well for both upland and waterfowl is the Wirehaired Pointing Griffon. They have a short bristly brown or gray coat that withstands water quite well. They are fairly small dogs.

Another pointer that works well is the German Wirehaired Pointer. With a coarse coat and whiskered face, the breed is basically a pointer, but can be trained to retrieve from water. Other hunters have Brittanies, German shorthairs and other breeds that turn in credible scores when conditions are right.

Which Breed Is Right For You?

Regardless of which breed you choose, the most important factor is choosing a dog you can enjoy and handle easily. Before you begin your search for a hunting dog, take a look at yourself. Consider your likes and dislikes. How much patience do you have? Under what conditions do you do most of your hunting? Do you have a quick temper? Will the dog be asked to do double duty as a watch dog? Will it live with you in the house or in its own kennel?

After answering these questions, talking to some of your fellow hunters with dogs, considering what you're willing to spend and conferring with some breeders, you should have a pretty good idea of which breed will suit you best.

Buying Your Dog

For most hunters, acquiring a dog usually means getting a puppy at a very young age. As soon as the dog is weaned is the best time to

The best way to decide which hunting dog is right for you is to consider the conditions you hunt the most and the lifestyle the dog will have at home.

acquire a puppy. Then both you and the puppy can start off properly.

You can, of course, acquire an older waterfowling dog, one that has already been trained. There are many excellent dogs with owners that have decided to give up hunting, for various reasons. Many of these older dogs are excellent and can be mighty happy if given the chance to hunt again. It does, however, occasionally take a refresher training course to get them back into the harness.

But seeing as most retrievers are acquired as puppies, the next step is to decide how and by whom the dog is going to be trained. You can have the puppy trained by experts, or you can do the job yourself. Following are suggestions from trainer Jack Nelson.

Training Your Own Retriever-The Basics

In most instances, training your own puppy is not particularly hard to do. It's fun, and the puppy and you become closer companions than if the dog was trained by someone else. There is however, one very important thing you must do. If you decide to train the puppy yourself, you must devote the necessary time it takes to do the job right. And it does take time. Not a lot of hours are required. In fact, a few moments a day is all that is needed. But this must be done *every day* to properly train your dog. You *must* make this commitment if you are going to properly train your retriever.

Obedience Training. Training your retriever to obey is the single most important facet of his training. A gun dog must, above all else, be obedient. The dog must be trained to sit or lie still on command in a boat, blind or out in the field, while there are extremely exciting things going on around him.

Probably the single worst habit of retrievers is breaking to ducks or geese coming in to the decoys. It's a natural instinct for the dog to chase birds. He must be taught regardless of what is around him to sit or lie still until commanded to do otherwise. Teaching the dog to properly enter a kennel, car, blind or boat is also important and can mean the difference in a frustrating or enjoyable day for all. Once you get the dog properly trained to obedience you can start refining his natural ability to retrieve.

The obedience commands the dog should learn are: *sit, stay, down, come, heel and kennel up.*

Sit. The first command to be taught is the word *sit.* Say the word "*sit,*" and gently, but firmly push down on the dog's hind quarters. Don't punish him if he doesn't do it, just keep repeating the step. Eventually he will do it without the hand pressure.

Stay. After teaching the dog to sit, the next step is *stay.* Place a

Most of the breeds noted for retrieving skills are intelligent dogs. Training them is not difficult, and with some patience it's a lot of fun.

It won't be long and you'll be able to move on to training your dog for real hunting conditions.

choke collar on the dog and tie it to a spot where you wish to command him to stay. Command him to *stay* and walk away from him. Repeat until he will stay without being tied in position.

After you get him to stay, command *sit*, then *stay*. When he will obey those commands without being tied in place, you're ready to start making him stay in place while throwing out retrieving dummies. After the dog is holding good, move some distance away from him, give the commands and have someone else throw out the dummies.

Down. Quite similar to sit, the command *down*, however, teaches the dog to lie down. This is extremely important for a water dog because you will wish him to lie down in a blind or boat to help break up his outline.

With the dog sitting, command *down* and pull his front feet out from under him, forcing him to lie down. Repeat until he will do it on his own, without your physical help.

Come. The next step is to teach your retriever to come to you when called. Place a choke collar and a long leash on the dog. First give the commands to *sit-stay*, then walk away from him. Give the command to *come* and gently tug on the leash. Don't at any time move towards the animal. Instead, always make sure he comes to you.

Heel. This is a very important command. Place the choke collar and leash on the dog and walk holding the dog by your side. Hold him in position as you issue the command *heel*. If he keeps walking in front of you swing the leash in an arc so it will hit him on the nose as he steps ahead of you.

Kennel Up. *Kennel up* is also a very important command. It makes it much easier to handle your retriever in the boat, car, etc. The best method is to first attach a long leash and choker collar on the dog, then get in the truck or automobile, etc. Give the command *kennel up*, and pat the floor of the vehicle. At the same time give a sharp tug on the leash holding the dog. Don't make the animal jump very high the first few times. That can come later. Once the dog learns to enter with you inside the vehicle, step outside and repeat the command until he learns to enter the vehicle on his own.

Gun Training. All gun dogs should receive gun training. This assures they will not become gun-shy, the nemesis of all gun dogs. The training is simple and easy. You should start them as young as possible, and introduce the sound of gunshot very gradually. Produce the sound while the dog is eating. Start with a cap pistol some distance away and gradually decrease the distance. You can then move to pistol blanks and finally a shotgun. A better method is to take your gun and a training dummy afield. Shoot the gun and toss the dummy for the pup to retrieve. He soon learns to associate the sound of the gun with the fun and excitement of retrieving.

Retrieving

Once your retriever has mastered the basics of obedience you can proceed with the advanced classes of learning to retrieve. This, again, should be a fun exercise for both you and the dog.

Advanced retrieving teaches the dog to interpret hand signals, how to mark ducks and how to retrieve them to hand. All the first lessons should be done on land, then you can introduce the dog to retrieving from water.

Basic Retrieving. The first step, of course, is to teach the dog to retrieve. With most water dogs this won't be any problem at all. The trick is to teach him to retrieve what, when and where you want him too.

Command the dog to *stay*, then give the command *mark*. At the same time toss a dummy away from him. Do not let him move from *stay*, and make sure that he sees the tossed dummy. Then issue the command *fetch* or *go*, whichever you wish to use, and push him toward the dummy. Once he picks up the dummy issue the command *come*. Make sure he brings the dummy all the way back to you. Then command him to *sit*. Take the dummy from him and make sure you give him lots of praise.

If he drops the dummy, and most do on the first attempts, put it back in his mouth. Hold the dummy in place in his mouth until you give the command *release*. Then take the dummy from him.

After the pup learns to retrieve a dummy on command toss out two dummies and teach him to bring each one back. Many trainers like to introduce live birds at this time. A pigeon will work, however a live mallard with wings shackled is the best to use.

Teaching Hand Signals. Once the puppy learns to retrieve properly, the next step is to teach him to take a line, or hand signal directing him towards the fallen bird. This takes time and practice but is a lot of fun for both teacher and student if done correctly.

The first step is to make the dog heel as you walk into the field. Then drop a dummy and continue walking for about 30 to 40 yards. Stop, make the dog sit. Then say *fetch* or *go*, and give him a forward motion with your hand to signal him to go. This teaches him to start off on your hand signals.

After he learns that, make him sit. Walk away from him a ways.

In the field the time spent training will pay off in a well-trained dog who's a real asset to you and your hunting partners.

Give the command *mark*, and throw the dummy over his head. Then say *back* and wave your hand towards the dummy. Once you get him retrieving behind himself, then throw the dummy to either side and motion with your hand, saying *mark*, then *back* each time.

Once the dog learns to retrieve on hand signals on land, then it's time to introduce him to water retrieving. This, again, can be fun for both the hunter and retriever. Merely toss the dummy into the water and repeat the lessons learned on land.

Sage Advice

I would like to add that there are many books and tapes on teaching advanced retrieving that can go into more detail than I can here, and I would suggest you might wish to use some of those to help send your retriever to ''college.''

Caring For Your Retriever

Waterfowling dogs get a tremendous workout during the season, and should be kept in top shape. It's a good idea to make sure you give the dog plenty of exercise all year. If you can combine it with some fun field work such as retrieving dummies from water, you're going to be well ahead of the game. Then, at least a full month before the season starts, give him at least 15 to 20 minutes a day full exercise to strengthen him for the coming season.

Make sure you match the dog's age to the chore, and don't forget to have vet check-ups before the season for older dogs.

10

Clothing and Other Gear

There are only two rules that must be remembered about water-fowling clothing. First the clothing must be a dull color or one that won't spook wary waterfowl, and secondly they must keep the hunter warm and dry.

There has always been special clothing made for waterfowlers, but today's hunters really have it great compared to those even a half dozen years ago. Modern fabrics and insulating materials are light-weight, easy-to-wear and shoot-with, and will keep a waterfowler warm and dry in the worst weather imaginable. Plus, they come in numerous camouflage patterns to suit almost any hunting situation.

Gore-Tex

Probably one of the most important developments has been the creation of Gore-Tex, by the Gore Company. Gore-Tex is a thin membrane of Teflon-based material that is sandwiched between a tough outer fabric layer and a thin soft inner fabric layer. The result is a windproof, waterproof, breathable fabric that allows moisture from inside to escape, yet prevents outside moisture from entering. Gore-Tex membrane has nine billion tiny pores per square inch. Each of these tiny pores is 20,000 times smaller than individual water droplets. This provides the waterproofing quality. On the oth-er hand, the pores are 700 times larger than water molecules in the vapor state, which allows for breathability.

Gore-Tex clothing allows moisture that is created by perspiration to escape instead of condensing on the inside of your clothing, yet rain and snow can not penetrate.

The membrane and fabric are impervious to contamination of body oils and are easily cleaned by machine washing with powder detergent. They are best drip dried, or tumble dried on low heat.

There is a wide variety of waterfowl clothing made by the various outdoor clothing manufacturers. These include waterfowlers' jackets, parkas, coveralls, and rain suits. The outer shell used in the manufacturer of the different items varies according to the use. This includes many specialty fabrics that are tough, long wearing and attractive, yet light in weight.

In addition to the moisture proof fabrics, the invention of manmade insulating materials has also helped create entirely new lines of waterfowling clothing. Down, the prime natural insulating material, is still preferred by many traditional waterfowlers, and no one will argue its heat retaining characteristics. However, it does have several disadvantages compared to many of the modern insulating materials.

One, it is much more bulky. Two, it becomes soggy and waterlogged when wet, which can be extremely dangerous to waterfowlers. And three, it costs quite a bit more than most manmade insulating materials.

The new man-made insulating materials, such as Thinsulate by the 3M Company, are made of extremely fine micro fibers. These create almost twice the thermal resistance as the same thickness of down. They are also breathable, durable, and are easily washed or dry cleaned. They absorb very little water, so they can keep you dry and warm even in extremely wet conditions.

Unfortunately, there are a number of cheap, imitation insulating materials that are not as good as the brand names. They cost less, but don't perform as well. Stick to clothing wearing the tags of name brand insulating materials. Thinsulate, Sontique and Quallofil, are all names to remember while shopping for hunting clothes. There are any number of waterfowling garments that incorporate these modern materials. I've tested those from Columbia and Walls and found them to be excellent.

Match Your Clothing To Your Hunting

Regardless of all else, you must match your clothing needs to your hunting situation and the climate in your area. For instance, if most of your hunting is in warm climates such as along much of the West

Many manufacturers are turning out high quality waterfowling garments which incorporate modern fabrics and insulations. Here Bob Allen wears his company's Squaw Creek system.

Coast, or down in the deep South, you will probably need lightweight, waterproof clothing. On the other hand, if your hunting is on the open bays of the Northeastern coast, or on ice covered inland lakes in the Midwest you'll need extra heavy clothing to provide protection from the weather.

Clothing Coloration

Another thing that must be taken into consideration is the coloration of the clothing. Again, there are numerous types of camouflage color patterns available for waterfowlers. Choose the ones that best suit the native vegetation in the area you are hunting. You may need several different patterns to match various hunting conditions, as well as the change in coloration from the early part of the season through the last.

Although there are many varieties, there are just four basic colors; dull green, sometimes called army green, brown or "dead grass", gray or black, simulating the coloration of tree trunks, and white that is used for field shooting in snow conditions or when hunting snow geese. The various greens can be used quite effectively early in the season when hunting green timber or much of the southern portion of the country. The most popular waterfowling color and pattern, however, is the "marsh grass" or brown. There are also several varieties of this, but all will do quite well in most waterfowling situations throughout most of the season. They blend especially well with

White coveralls are a good choice when hunting on snow covered terrain or hunting snow geese from the middle of a decoy spread.

marsh hunting conditions, but also break up your outline when boat hunting as well.

A relatively new innovation are the gray and black patterns made to resemble a tree trunk. These can be extremely effective in hunting situations where you are hunting in timber. This includes green-timber hunting, as well as hunting the flooded reservoirs that have dead standing timber in them. I have had very good success in the latter case merely standing next to a dead snag in a shallow cove, and calling mallards within a dozen yards.

Layered Clothing

In many parts of the country, a day in the marsh can have a variety of conditions. You may start off early in the morning with cold, damp conditions and a skim of ice on the water. By noon, however, the weather may be almost shirt-sleeve warm.

The only solution is to wear layered clothing. This way you can remove layers as needed to prevent overheating.

Wearing layered clothing is important for extreme cold weather hunting as well. The layers of clothing help provide more insulation for body heat. If they are of the correct materials they will also allow perspiration and moisture to escape. A build up of moisture next to the skin can be deadly under such conditions.

Underwear

The first layer is underwear. Most waterfowling conditions require the use of ''long'' underwear for extra warmth and protection. Avoid underwear made from cotton because it absorbs perspiration and holds it.

One of the best cold-weather underwear combinations is the fishnet, or mesh, underwear under a pair of regular ''longjohns'' or cotton lined wool type. Fishnet underwear provides dead air spaces to retain body heat. The outer layer traps it.

Another good choice these days is underwear made with some of the new man-made fabrics like Thermolactyl, which is a combination of Vinyon and acrylic. Experiments done in the severe climatic conditions of Greenland have shown the fabric to be superior to classic natural fibers in both insulating power and heat retention. There is a wide variety of underwear styles using this material made exclusively by the Damart Company. It's only a matter of choosing the one that best suits your needs.

Polypropylene is another fine material for the layer next to your body. It hates moisture and wicks it away from your skin.

Second Layer

Over the inner underwear layer goes the second layer. This should be light-weight, but tough. It should also allow body moisture to escape. There are any number of different clothing items made for this purpose. Ideally they should be made out of wool, which traps a lot of dead air space, so it insulates well. It also retains some of its insulating qualities even when it gets wet, something especially valuable to waterfowl hunters.

I like to wear a pair of thick wool pants underneath my waders when hunting during cold weather. They are more comfortable than blue jeans, plus they provide better protection against the leaks I didn't know were there.

Most of the shirts and sweaters I wear are also made out of wool. The tightly knit ones wear better than the fuzzy ones, but don't offer as much heat retention. Loose, almost baggy clothing is warmer than tight fitting items.

One item that is good for this layer is the turtleneck sweater. It can be invaluable in keeping not only your neck warm, but your torso as well. It is estimated that fifty percent or more of the heat radiated from the body escapes from the head and neck region. A turtleneck prevents some of that heat from escaping.

Outer Layer

The final, outer layer can consist of any number of different items, again depending on the hunting situation. For fairly mild weather you could probably get by with a light-weight hunting jacket. For foul weather you may need a heavy duty parka, or even an insulated hunting suit or coveralls. Coveralls are a disadvantage at times, because they don't lend themselves to the versatility of layering. They're either all on or all off.

An interesting trend is the growing number of "combination" outer wear garments. These combine a number of different layers to provide comfort throughout the day when hunting during a period of weather changes.

One of the leaders in this type of design was the Quad Parka from Columbia Sportswear. It features a Gore-Tex shell for protection against rain. Inside is a removable, reversible Thinsulate liner featuring two camo patterns. Either piece can be worn separately or zipped together, allowing waterfowlers versatility in their clothing choices. Other companies producing similar high-quality parkas include Bob Allen, Remington, Fieldline, Walls, 10X, RealTree and others.

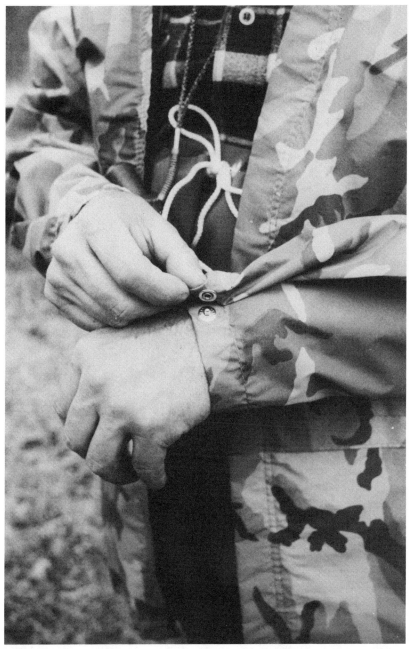

When choosing rainwear, look for conveniences like snaps at the cuffs. You'll find that you'll be wearing quality rain gear under many conditions.

Rain Gear

For extremely wet weather you will need good rain gear. This should be constructed of the toughest, light-weight material you can find. It should also have provisions for allowing body moisture to escape. On coats and parkas, this usually means an opening along the back or under the arms that is lined with a plastic mesh or other material that lets moisture out. High-quality raingear will also have elastic cuffs at the wrists to keep out snow and rain, and a drawstring hood for more protection. Legs should have snap cuffs or zippers to allow for easy on and off over boots, yet help keep out moisture.

In some cases, you'll find that you're wearing your quality raingear even when conditions are dry but windy. A waterproof outer layer does a great job at cutting a cold prairie wind.

Socks

The biggest problem most waterfowlers face is cold feet. It can be avoided by wearing the right kind of socks. Avoid socks with high cotton content. Wool socks insulate much better. The new manmade fabrics also make excellent socks. They help "wick" moisture away from your feet, keeping them dry and warm.

One final tip. Wear two pair of socks. Most boots run a bit larger than regular shoes and an extra pair will make them fit more comfortably.

Boots

Boots, of course, are a very important part of waterfowling. Make certain the ones you're wearing match the hunting situation precisely. Wet feet have ruined more than one waterfowler's day afield.

Field hunters have it the easiest. They can usually get by with a pair of waterproof leather or short rubber boots. In extremely muddy conditions, hip boots are the way to go. They provide a little extra "margin of error" in case you hit a hole that's deeper than you expected. Those hunting exclusively from a boat can also sometimes get by with ankle-length boots too, though hip boots or chest waders come in handy at times.

Hip boots are good for most shallow water walk-in hunting situations. Trouble is, shallow water rarely stays shallow. Regardless if there is guaranteed to be only knee-deep water I'll find a deep hole, so I always wear chest waders in any waterfowl wading situations. I have found they are the best way to avoid getting wet.

There is one important fact concerning chest waders. Buy the best quality, name brand waders you can afford. There is nothing more

Traditional waders and hip boots come in a variety of materials and with varying levels of insulation. If you stick with name brands, the boots should last many years with just a bit of care.

startling than icy water seeping down your legs from a puncture in your waders. Although it can happen to good waders too, especially when they get older, when it comes to waders you usually get what you pay for. The better quality ones last longer than the cheaper ones. Most waterfowling conditions are cold, so insulated waders are the best choice.

These days you can purchase waders suited not only to your foot size, but your stature as well. This is good news for hunters who are taller or shorter than the average hunter.

You will also need a good pair of suspenders for your waders, and knowledgeable hunters also wear a belt around the middle of their waders. This is especially important when boating or wearing them in areas where you might accidentally get into deep water. The belt prevents the waders from filling up with water should you step over their tops. If you should get into this kind of trouble, belted waders will actually provide floatation because of the trapped air.

One of the biggest problems with waders, both hip and chest styles, is the inevitable cracks and creases that form in them. Both rubber and plastic are organic materials, meaning they come from plant life. Natural rubber comes from rubber tree sap and synthetic rubber and plastics come from coal and oil. Cracking and oxidation are natural aging processes as is exposure to ozone and tension caused by folding or binding the material.

Over the years, many waterfowlers have discovered ingenious ways for hanging their boots up so there is no stress on them during the off season. But, according to the Marathon Rubber Company, the best method of assuring long life for your boots is too eliminate

Neoprene is a very popular and comfortable material for waders. The one drawback is that you'll need to buy wading boots too.

Keep waders stored in a light-tight, semi-air-tight box. This will reduce the effects of ozone on the rubber and prolong their lifespan.

exposure to ozone. Instead of hanging boots up, store them in an airtight bag, box or chest. Make sure the boots are dry inside to avoid mildewed linings. Loosely fold or roll the boots up before storing them away from light and ozone producing machinery such as electric motors.

Headgear

It has already been mentioned that approximately fifty percent or more of body heat is lost through the head and neck region. For that reason these areas should be extremely well protected during waterfowling, especially during foul weather. In cold, but dry weather, nothing beats a wool watch cap pulled down over your ears and the back of your neck. It can also be rolled up as needed for warmer weather. The only disadvantage is there is no bill to shade your eyes, and this can be a problem in bright sunlight. Newer versions also add the waterproofing capabilities of Gore-Tex to make really warm and moisture-proof headgear.

There are also a number of specialty waterfowlers' caps, ranging from the light-weight Jones style, to heavy duty Gore-Tex, and Thinsulate lined caps for cold and foul weather. These caps also have ear flaps that can fold down for extreme cold. All of the waterfowling caps are available in a variety of camouflage patterns.

Gloves

Bone-chilling cold weather also means gloves to most waterfowlers, and again there have been some interesting developments in hand gear as well. There are three necessities in waterfowling gloves: *warmth, ease of shooting,* and *water resistance.*

One of the biggest problems that have plagued waterfowlers for years is handling wet decoys in freezing weather. There have been a number of rubber gloves designed for the chore. The problem is that most are also cold and clumsy to work with. Special camouflaged waterfowling gloves these days made with Gore-Tex and Thinsulate such as those by Cabela's, offer the best of everything. They're light-weight, waterproof, and make it easy to handle complicated chores such as taking up decoys, etc.

Spare Clothing

More than once I've taken a dunking while waterfowling, and one rule I have adhered to for a long time is carrying a full set of extra clothes in my vehicle, including long underwear and plenty of extra socks. In some instances the only things I have to change during the day is my socks. In other instances, however, when the water is deeper than my boots are high, I'm glad to have the rest of the clothes.

Other Gear

There are also numerous other waterfowling items that can not only make your hunt more enjoyable, but safer and more successful.

Floatation Devises. When waterfowling from a boat, a personal floatation devise is mandatory. There are any number of specially made units for waterfowlers, including the Stearns Sans-Souci Sportvest Camouflaged Vest which offers waterfowlers full floatation plus plenty of pockets. Stearns also has floatation jackets and pants in a camouflage pattern. They offer full floatation and insulation for protection against hypothermia as well.

Floatation Suits. Serious big water waterfowlers should give consideration to investing in a complete floatation suit like those offered by Mustang Manufacturing. These garments are very warm and of course offer the ultimate in floatation if you find yourself in the water. These suits which incorporate special inflatable air chambers are not inexpensive. But the least they'll do is give you added confidence when you face rough water and they could end up saving your life.

Seats and Cushions. I discovered the pleasure of hunting with a foam seat while turkey hunting, and didn't take too long to decide it could add much more comfort to waterfowling as well. My seat, made by Lohman Manufacturing Company, is a camouflaged piece of foam complete with a strap. I take it everywhere. It reduces the discomfort from a day-long sit on a hard plank bench of a blind or the cold metal seat of a waterfowling boat.

Another item to consider bringing along is one of the many folding seats or combination seat/coolers. They are comfortable to sit on, and can be used to carry your lunch and beverages.

Staying Warm

Cold weather and waterfowling often go hand in hand, so one of the biggest chores is keeping warm. Even the best of clothing sometimes isn't enough. The answer is a variety of heaters that can be used. The first type is personal hand-warmers. A pair of these in your pockets not only provide instant warmth for your hands, but they also keep your torso warm. These are available as solid or liquid fuel and either one can take the chill off a cold day.

One of the best I have heard of is the Re-Heater pack. With the push of a button, these self-contained, reuseable packs heat to 130 degrees in 10 seconds and last for a couple hours. Back at home, you simply boil them for 20 minutes or so, and they are ready to go again. No fuel of any sort is ever needed.

Another heater to consider is the bigger space heater. There are a number of portable catalytic or kerosene heaters that can be used to heat a blind or boat for warmer, more comfortable waterfowling. Make sure your blind is well ventilated before using them, however, because they use oxygen while burning.

Carrying Gear

One thing waterfowlers have is lots of gear, regardless of whether they're hiking back into a remote slough or boating across a lake to an island. There are numerous ways of carrying items such as a jug of coffee or hot chocolate, shells, extra clothes, cameras, guns etc. For small items a fanny pack can be ideal. For larger items you can go as big as you desire. I often carry large numbers of cameras into a blind or area, and have found nothing beats a pack frame for packing in cameras and gear. It leaves my hands free for carrying my gun, and for holding a wading staff if necessary.

For decoys, there are a number of decoy bags available. Look for ones that are strong and absorb little water.

Miscellaneous Items

There are also numerous small, miscellaneous items you may wish to take along on your trips. Flashlights, light-weight binoculars, a camera, and knives all come in handy at times. A good item to

A simple stool like this one can help carry a lot of gear and make a day in a cramped blind much more comfortable.

bring is an emergency survival kit complete with waterproof matches.

Indeed, collecting gear for waterfowling is one of the major enjoyments for many hunters. With the right gear and clothing, waterfowling can be a joy, with the wrong kind utter frustration, and sometimes downright dangerous.

11

Duck Hunting Strategies

The essence of duck hunting, for many sportspersons, is tradition. Really it's that way in all types of hunting. How else can you explain the surge of popularity in black powder guns and bows. Seemingly as far back as all of time, man has hunted ducks for food. Only more recently for sport.

But beyond tradition, today's waterfowler enjoys his sport for the variety it offers. That's everything from zipping teal over a flooded rice field to scoters in the crashing ocean surf! It's the fondest hope of most waterfowl hunters that they'll experience each variation and species sometime during their years afield.

Because of the wide variety of species and situations, each requires its own special techniques and strategies. Let's take a look at several of them so you'll be more prepared when you encounter a new situation and as a refresher course on the basics you may already know.

Early Season Teal Hunting

Teal and a few other species migrate, for the most part, earlier in the fall than the main migration flights of most species. For this reason, many states offer a special teal season which runs for several days about a week to a month ahead of the main duck season.

These seasons are often termed "bonus seasons" by the state fish & game departments, and that sums up the hunting situation.

Success depends on two factors: 1)*the timing of the migration* and 2)*the local weather/water conditions.* There is simply no way to predict teal when the teal will be where, even if the season is open on them!

The single best tactic is to look for them, rather than sit in a traditional regular season hot spot and wait for them to come to you.

As a rule, teal flights start in late August, peaking in September with most of the bluewings through by late October. Of course, this depends on the weather, the season and what part of the country in which you are hunting.

On the other hand, green-winged teal start their migration a bit later and peak in late October or early November. So for the most part, it's the bluewings that provide the shooting during the early teal seasons.

The season is always a hit or miss situation. If you have good water conditions and flights of teal corresponding to the open season dates, then you have good hunting. If the flights are off the season a bit, or there is no water, then teal hunting will be quite dismal.

The main problem with early season teal is that the ducks key on shallow water areas. The majority of these are simply dry or mud flats during the early part of the season when the birds come through. Most parts of the country are somewhat dry by the end of the summer and haven't yet received the annual fall rains by the start of the teal season.

In addition, many public waterfowling areas as well as the majority of private duck lakes across the country, are managed for water levels to increase around mid-October. Therefore, there are simply not a lot of areas with the right conditions to attract teal during the early season.

Oh, but if the season is wet and the birds come in at the right time, be sure you're stocked up on Number 6 steel loads. Good water holds the birds well, and shooting will be fantastic!

Prospecting is the key to bettering your odds for a successful teal season. Again, some of the best places to look for these early ducks are small potholes, ponds, backwaters of creeks, sloughs, flooded river bottoms, stock tanks and flooded rice fields.

Many of the best locations will be on private land and, of course, you'll need specific permission to hunt them.

The best shallow water areas will have flooded vegetation. These little ducks generally move through so fast, they are primarily interested in resting sights rather than using them as feeding spots like late season ducks will.

The success of the early teal seasons are most often dictated by stage of the migration and local water conditions.

Green timber hunting presents thrills that are unique in waterfowling. Every hunter should have the chance to experience them at least once.

Hunting teal during the early season will take every bit of general waterfowl hunting skill you can muster, plus a good bunch of luck. This includes good shooting to hit these small and speedy targets.

Most important is proper identification! Flights of teal may be mixed with a number of other small ducks including woodies, shovelers, gadwalls and others. Sometimes the immature birds will not yet be in full plumage, and this can make identification even more difficult. Both for the sake of your conscience and the trouble you can get in, *be absolutely sure you know what you're shooting at before you pull the trigger!*

Teal hunting can be done over decoys in shallow water. If water conditions are low, you can usually flush a flight from an area, set up your spread and have them come right back. But if water is abundant, they'll probably just move on to a new area. One great thing about early teal hunting is that it's generally done in comfortable weather. It makes a great tune-up for your retriever before the real work begins!

Jump shooting is another popular technique for taking teal. Either wading or hunting from a canoe on a winding river can provide fast action.

That's teal hunting! You pretty much have to make your own success by finding the birds, if they're around to be found. But it's a great way to add a week to our too short waterfowling year!

Green Timber Hunting

Some of waterfowling's most exciting challenges are found in the timbered flats of flooded river bottom land. Unfortunately, there is a dwindling supply of this kind of terrain and fewer hunters have the opportunity to experience this kind of thrilling hunt.

Today, the majority of remaining green timber hunting exists in the Grand Prairie region of Arkansas around the world famous duck town of Stuttgart. Other green timber terrain is available in the U.S., but it is quite scattered. Most are in private hands and relatively small compared to the huge tracts hunted at the turn of the century.

Some states, particularly in the South, are trying to preserve and refurbish green timber habitat for ducks. It's prime waterfowl country and deserves every chance we can give it!

The flooding of the timbered bottoms provides a shallow "sheet" of water throughout thousands of acres of nut producing trees such as oaks and pecans. Mallards, pintails and other puddle ducks swarm into these floating smorgasbords like flies to honey. Each year the water recedes and allows the trees to continue growing, rather than drown them as happens on reservoirs. However, the first couple years on a new reservoir will provide a similar situation.

But on to the hunting!

Green timber hunting is simple and exciting. It doesn't take a lot of gear. And even the novice can experience thrilling shooting if he puts himself in the right place at the right time.

Good callers have the distinct advantage in hunting flooded timber. Since the birds won't see a decoy spread until they are very close, calling virtually alone must be relied upon to attract them. Even huge flocks can be called in!

All you'll really need is a good pair of chest waders, a handful of decoys and a good call, but some hunters prefer to tow along a small boat to hold decoys, dog, guns, lunch, etc.

Hunting is not done from a blind or the boat, but simply standing next to the base of a tree. Stay on the shadow side of the tree, don't move to much, and the ducks will never know you're there. Some hunters like to take along a miniature tree seat like a deer hunter might use. Screwed into the side of a tree trunk, it can provide a comfortable place for you or your dog to sit.

Sometimes blinds are used on private areas, but for the most part, hunters watch for flights of feeding mallards, then hunt the area being used at the time.

Green timber hunting does offer some advantages to the beginning caller, too. The fact that you won't be calling ducks from a great distance is a real help. About the only call you'll need is the feeding chatter mixed with a few solitary quacks. As the situation warrants, and experience will tell you, you may wish to use the "sit-down" call as well.

In most instances you won't be able to see the ducks until they're almost on top of you. Listening carefully may give you an extra second's warning before the ducks come into sight. Also, watch your dog. His sensitive ears will pick up the sound of approaching flocks before yours will.

If you're in the right spot, you just can't keep the mallards from coming in. As an added attractor, many hunters like to swish their feet around to create a disturbance in the water, further convincing nearby ducks that other feeding ducks are in the area.

Green timber shooting calls for an open-choked shotgun! When a flight of mallards decides to come into a green tree set they simply drop from the sky! I've seen over 1,000 mallards start a funnel and land within a couple dozen yards of where some mighty excited, not so quiet hunters stood wide-eyed in disbelief.

Then when on the flush, birds go in every direction! They head straight for the tree tops and go! And that makes for some mighty sporty shotgunning!

Green timber mallards are something every waterfowl hunter should experience at least once in his lifetime.

Marsh Hunting

Traditionally, the majority of duck hunting in this country has been for mallards and other puddle ducks on the numerous marshes. With the continued draining of wetlands and the damming of rivers, this has been changing.

It's still the most common duck hunting scenario, but the hunting is concentrated in fewer, smaller areas. A great deal of it is also on public lands, these days; and there is a lot of competition for relatively few ducks.

As with most waterfowling situations, marsh hunting techniques vary according to local situations and the species of ducks you're pursuing. A great deal depends on the size and type of marsh. If the marsh is large, ducks may spend their entire stay in its confines, both feeding and resting there. If the marsh is small, ducks may only rest there and spend a good part of the day feeding in nearby fields. Or some species are apt to feed in the marsh and spend their loafing hours on nearby open water.

Typically, marsh hunting is done with decoys and from a blind, either permanent or portable. Because of the popularity of these areas for ducks, as well as the tremendous hunting pressure they receive, you will usually be restricted to one portion of the marsh. This is regardless of whether it's public or private hunting property. You'll most likely have to share the area with other hunters.

If you do have the opportunity to pick your spot on the marsh, try to observe it for some time with binoculars. This will help you pinpoint which part of the area ducks are using most heavily. Also observe where they are coming from and where they are going. This should tell you if the birds are loafing or feeding or both. You may find that the wisest choice is to get away from the crowd of hunters and pursue the birds in the feeding fields a few miles away.

Observation will also reveal the best time to set up. Usually, the best marsh duck hunting comes right at day break when most waterfowl move from night time roosts to feeding areas. Once in the feeding areas, they may feed for only an hour or for most of the day depending on current and pending weather conditions.

Marsh hunting for ducks is probably the most common waterfowling scenario. You can make it as simple or complex as you want.

Success can be tough to come by in a crowded marsh hunting situation. That's what makes it so sweet.

Under mild conditions, the birds will feed in the morning, head back to rest through the middle of the day, then feed again in late afternoon. During periods of foul weather or with bad weather on the way, they may feed all day in preparation for a hasty move south.

Recognize that if the marsh you're hunting is primarily a resting area, the best hunting hours may be the middle of the day. No doubt there will be a lull after the early morning flights leave to feed, but the action at 10 or 11 o'clock could make it worth your sticking it out. Likewise, the last few moments of legal shooting are often worth staying for. Birds that have been on the afternoon feed will generally make every effort to get back to the marsh before real darkness settles. If you're there waiting for them, shooting can be great!

As mentioned in the chapter on decoys, the number and type of decoys to use is dependent upon the species and size of flocks using the area. It may also depend on how much other hunting competition there is on the marsh as well.

Most marsh hunting is in open potholes or small lakes that are natural or man-made. These small areas can quite easily become over-shot. Knowledgeable managers and hunters will permit hunting on these areas only in the morning. Left alone in the afternoon, they provide a safe resting area and confidence builders for the spooky ducks.

Whether on public or private land, it takes some serious scouting to find good marsh hunting opportunities, but the effort can be very rewarding. Don't rule out the idea of chartering a small plane for an hour or two in the early fall. The pilot can fly you over new country or a favorite old marsh to reveal hidden ponds and potholes that might be an untapped bonanza!

Some of the best marsh shooting may be next to a river channel so another good scouting method is by boating the river or by walking the banks. Watch for outflowing sloughs and small oxbow lakes and backwaters.

Regardless of whether it's a small pothole, with only a handful of ducks, or a huge marsh with hundreds of hunters, marsh shooting for ducks is still a tradition available for most waterfowlers to enjoy. Companionship, good hunting and simply a day in the marsh are the rewards for those willing to work to find a place to hunt.

Field Hunting Ducks

There isn't much a big ol' red-legged mallard likes better than corn! They'll hit a prime cornfield over most any other food source. And for the hunter with some savvy, this weakness will provide some challenging and productive shooting!

For the most part, ducks don't usually stay feed in a field continuously like geese do. They will, however, stay as long as there is a prime feed field like corn or soybeans. They particularly like one that is flooded.

They can be driven out by hunting pressure. Though most field goose and some field duck hunting is done from blinds, most field duck hunting is an opportunistic situation. The hunter spots ducks using a field and either makes a sneak on them, or sets up in the area to hunt them with decoys.

This is also an excellent technique to locate some mighty good hunting. The method can be used even in an area that is pretty well sewed up by private duck clubs.

Spend some time driving country roads and watch for ducks to come off the private clubs and head out to feed. Most likely you'll find a farmer who will be more than glad to have you harvest a few ducks that are gleaning his fields like miniature combines. This tactic is particularly good for grain fields around large lakes, rivers or waterfowl refuges.

In some instances, commercial duck hunting outfits plan fields to be flooded specifically for ducks and duck hunting clients. A flooded corn, soybean or picked rice field can prove heaven for a hunter. In these cases there are usually permanent or semi-permanent sunken blinds in the field to provide comfort as well as concealment.

When prospecting on your own, however, about the only thing you'll need is a dozen decoys, plenty of shells, waders or hip boots, and something to hide under. The ground can be wet, cold, soggy mud, so it's a good idea to take along a waterproof ground cloth or tarp to lay on. Perforated camouflage cloths make excellent "blinds" for this type of hunting.

River Hunting

Hunting the rivers is also an excellent way for the waterfowler who doesn't have the access or inclination to join a private duck hunting club.

Ducks are just naturally drawn to rivers. Regardless of whether they are huge, famous rivers or tiny, locally known creeks, all can provide some fast duck shooting. It does, however, take a bit more work to find them than some of the more popular hunting areas.

There are basically two methods of river hunting: 1)*locating on a sandbar or peninsula and calling passing birds into decoys* or *floating the river in hopes of sneaking within range of rafting or resting ducks*.

River sandbar hunting is a tradition in many parts of the country. The technique is much the same as hunting decoying ducks in marshes. In most instances, however, the river blinds are portable and are set up each day. These may be boat blinds, portable shore blinds or nothing more than camouflage cloth.

River sandbar hunting usually provides a greater opportunity to take different species than does marsh hunting, so most hunters pack along several species and sizes of decoys. These might include goose decoys if there are geese in the area.

River hunting can often provide action when other methods and techniques aren't working. It simply requires a little more work and careful adherence to safety precautions.

Floating a river or creek to sneak up on ducks is one of the most relaxing yet exciting methods of hunting ducks. The tactic is simple; the results fun and quite often productive. It also provides a chance

Drifting quietly down small rivers and streams can be a very effective system for ducks. Be careful when shooting from a boat.

to hunt in areas that are mostly private land. Different rules govern river navigation and trespassing in different states, so make sure you understand the rules in the area you plan to hunt.

Although you can often float the larger rivers quite easily, the smaller rivers provide the best opportunity to surprise a bunch of resting ducks. In fact, the tiny brush-lined creeks that will barely float a canoe are often the best bets. This is particularly so both early and late in the season. The best hunting hours are usually in the middle of the day when ducks have finished feeding and seek out these riverine hideaways.

The most productive rivers will be fairly quiet with lots of log jams and backwater pools. Because you'll have to portage quite a bit, the best boats to use are small, lightweight jon boats or better yet a canoe. In most instances, a dark or green boat will suffice, but you can also paint your boat with a camo pattern or simply throw a camouflage cloth over the front of it if you wish.

Most states prohibit shooting from a boat under power, so the technique is to drift down the river with the current. Make as little noise as possible and stay to the inside edge of bends. Usually when you come around a bend, there will be a quiet eddy on the inside and by sticking closely to that bank you'll be closer to any ducks resting on that pool.

River floating provides fast, close-in shooting. It's also quite challenging because of the flush of the ducks and the motion of the boat. You not only have to be quick on the trigger, but you have to be fast at identifying ducks you only see for a split-second before they flush and are gone.

In many instances, the birds will only fly 100 yards downstream then settle back down on the river. You may be able to ambush them again, but it will take even more stealth.

Although one person can successfully float a river, it's more fun and productive with two. The stern hunter navigates the boat or canoe while the bow hunter does the shooting. *Only the bow hunter should be allowed to shoot!* The hunters should alternate on a regular basis to give both an ample crack at the fun.

Sometimes it's possible to drift down a river, then motor back to your put-in point. If the river is of any size, and you intend to hunt a good section of it, the best method is to use two vehicles. Place one at the take-out point, then drive the second to the put-in point and start your hunt.

Whichever way you go about it, river hunting is a ball! As always be careful.

Sneak Hunting Ducks

Another good method of hunting waterfowl is the sneak. It works great for birds on potholes and farm ponds.

Sneak hunting not only provides some very exciting and productive hunting, but does so without the expense of maintaining a private duck lake and gear such as decoys, boats, etc. All it requires is a pair of waders, a gun, the right shells, a pair of binoculars and an old fishing rod or a long cord with a weight and a hook to retrieve kills. Or you can take along your trusty retriever if he's trained to heel perfectly.

Sneak hunting is particularly good for teal and other early migrating species, but it's worth trying right through to the final days of the season.

Regardless of how much food and habitat is available, it doesn't take ducks long to become wary of the high hunting pressure on big marshes and lakes. Smart ducks soon learn that thousands of tiny potholes and farm ponds are rarely used by hunters. Dumb ones die quickly!

Many out of the way water areas are rarely visited by anyone. More than once I've flushed hundreds of birds from a pond no bigger than the average backyard swimming pool.

The first step to enjoying this type of hunting is to locate a number of potholes or ponds that might be good resting places for ducks. I've discovered a number of these while quail hunting. Before the strict steel shot regulations went into effect, I always carried a few heavy loads in my pocket while following my bird dogs. When a promising pond loomed ahead, I'd call the dogs to heel, pop the heavy loads in the chambers and have a go at it. More than once I brought home the bacon, so to speak!

One good method of locating promising ponds is to check with the local or county agricultural extension office. They often have a list of landowners who may have impoundments and allow hunting on them. You can also check with the local fish and game officer as well.

Again, a good scouting method is to hire a small plane for a few hours. You'll discover many hidden hotspots that aren't visible from the road.

From then on, it's a matter of obtaining permission to hunt. Although many landowners won't allow other types of hunting, you can quite often get the go ahead for a duck hunt. This is especially true when dealing with farmers who have sustained crop losses caused by waterfowl.

Sneaking up on potholes and farm ponds combines duck hunting with the skills big game hunters often use.

It may get you a few disbelieving stares, but a fishing rod and a top-water lure can aid in retrieving birds downed in deep water.

Once you get a good number of ponds located along with permission to hunt, the hunting is easy.

The best time to sneak hunt is during the middle of the day, so you won't have to get up at the crazy hours marsh hunters do. You can go about your sport at more civilized hours of the day.

If possible, view the pond from a distance with binoculars before making your sneak. This way you can determine where the ducks are located on the pond. With that in mind, you can plan your sneak to get as close as possible before revealing yourself to the birds. A successful sneak on a fairly open pond is a stratagem in which you can take pride!

If you can't observe the pond first, you will have to make a blind sneak. This can be exciting, but usually not as productive. It's merely a matter of sneaking up the dam side of the pond. Move as slowly and quietly as possible. When you're next to the top edge, raise your head just a little at a time and observe as much water area as possible, then raise it a bit more and scan more of the pond area.

Regardless of how careful you are, the flush will probably be startling. Sometimes it works best to have two hunters on larger ponds. You can make a sort of pincer movement to trap ducks between you. In this manner, at least one hunter will get some shooting even if the birds flush wild.

The biggest problem with sneak hunting comes after the shooting. It's retrieving ducks that fall in water too deep to wade. This is where the old fishing rod comes in handy.

Equip the rod with a heavy top-water lure or treble hook and weight. Simply cast past the fallen duck, swing your line over it and retrieve your bird. If you wait long enough the fallen birds will drift in to shore, but the rod and reel trick speeds things up and lets you get on to the next sneak hunting site.

Like in float hunting, instant identification is a must for the sneak hunter. But with that skill well in hand, sneak hunting is a great way of producing "off hours" action.

Hunting Open Water And Large Lakes

Probably the most demanding duck hunting is done on the coastal bays and flats and on huge inland lakes and reservoirs.

Without exception, this type of waterfowl hunting demands the best of everything; boats, gear, clothing, wingshooting, knowledge of duck habits and identification, boating skills and intestinal fortitude.

The bread and butter of the big water hunter are the diver species, with some of the hardier puddlers thrown in for a change of pace. Unlike the feeding and loafing patterns ducks exhibit on inland marshes and backwaters, diving ducks and sometimes puddle ducks will raft up on these huge expanses of water, often feeding all day on aquatic vegetation. This is especially true of divers which go to some depth for their favorite delicacies.

There are several methods of hunting these huge flights of ducks including decoying them from various blind locations and sneaking on them with low-profile boats.

Decoying Open Water Ducks. Locating a blind and decoy set on a rocky point or on the lee side of an island is an extremely effective method of hunting these large open water areas. It takes a big set of decoys to bring in these huge flights, and the weather and water can be quite rough. Other than those factors, you can use much of the same basic knowledge that applies to inland hunting.

Off shore open water sets, however, are a different matter. As shown in the decoy chapter of this book, there is a difference in how these sets are made compared to marsh sets. It also takes huge numbers of dekes to make these spread effective.

The decoys must be rigged around a permanent stake blind or more often around floating blinds or boat blinds like a layout boat. It takes hardy hunters and good seamanship to brave the heavy weather and seas one experiences in this kind of hunting. The methods, however, are rooted in tradition because they are so effective.

Sneaking Open Water Ducks. Another method of hunting open water is sneaking up on rafting ducks using special boats like the sneak box or the sculling boat.

For many years the sculling boat was a very popular type of waterfowling boat. Then it just sort of faded away, kept alive by a few diehard traditionalists on the East Coast. But recently, this type of waterfowling has seen a resurgence in popularity, and sculling boats are again being manufactured and used.

The tactic is simple and effective. The gunner lies down in the flat, wedge-shaped boat and uses a single big oar protruding from the stern to propel the boat forward. It takes time and patience to slowly move the boat in close enough to provide shooting, but the results can be exciting and effective. Of course, when you're beginning a sneak in a scull boat you'll find it easiest if you can maneuver into position to allow the wind to help push you toward the unsuspecting fowl.

Reservoirs. With the large number of Corps of Engineers Reservoirs across the country and their resulting public hunting lands and waters, it's only fitting that we discuss tactics for hunting them. Some of the best hunting in the country is now on these man-made bodies.

Reservoirs are typically red hot waterfowling areas when they are first built, and then gradually taper off as vegetation dies and falls into the lake.

If the terrain of the lake encompasses a lot of shallow mud flats was well as an expanse of bordering marsh, they can provide fabulous hunting for many, many years. Many of these lakes are drawn down by late summer and aquatic/semi-aquatic plants grow on the mud flats. Then when the fall rains come, they are submerged providing a smorgasbord for waterfowl.

For the most part, however, these lakes are used primarily as resting areas for ducks, and they'll fly to nearby grain fields to do their actual feeding. The best hunting is then from about mid-morning through mid-day as ducks come back from feeding and mill about looking for good resting areas. It takes a good number of decoys on these big bodies of water to assure that birds will decide to raft with your set.

Because of the variety of terrain these lakes usually encompass, they quite often provide a tremendous variety of hunting conditions as well as species of ducks to hunt. Most reservoirs include small

This is what late season waterfowling is all about. The weather's at its worst, shooting at its best.

feeder creeks, surrounding marshlands of shallow mud flats and deep open water with underwater vegetation. For information concerning hunting in the lakes in your area, contact the nearest Army Corps of Engineers office.

Hunting Late Season Ducks

When it comes to duck hunting, the very end of the season is often the very best. The majority of the birds will be migrating at this time and you may have the hunting pretty much to yourself.

It takes a lot of good equipment, some patience and a bunch of intestinal fortitude to withstand the freezing temperatures and rough weather of late season in much of the country. But if you stick it out, you'll find that most hunters will have quit the fields by that time, or at least switched to hunting other species.

Because much of the previously open water may be frozen,

In late season, concentrate on any patches of open water no matter how small.

ducks will usually become very concentrated in smaller areas. When you find them, the shooting will be more than enough to keep you warm! Quite often, you can't drive them away from a particular patch of open water when everything else in the area is frozen solid.

Any pond of open water can be a drawing card. All you have to do is find it! Check spring fed sections of large lakes and small creeks or rivers with open pools. Regardless, find it and you'll have all the shooting you desire!

You can also try breaking ice in the potholes if it's not to thick. A couple days of this and the ducks will find you. In fact, you probably won't even need any decoys. The open water will be lure enough to get them to pitch right in.

Of course, you'll need to take special precautions to protect yourself from the worst the elements can dish out. *Bundle up!* Hypothermia is the biggest killer of waterfowl hunters!

The one drawback to this type of hunting is the birds that you find in late season migrate like the hounds of hell are behind them! They will be here today, gone tomorrow. They won't linger like their early season brethren.

But if you can find open water and be there at the right time, those final hours of the season will likely give you enough memories to keep your heart pounding right on through the off-season!

Bill Harper knows that when it all comes together, it feels real good.

12

Goose Hunting Strategies

Far too many geese have fallen to waterfowl hunters whose primary targets were ducks for anyone to conclude that you can't take the big birds by the same methods. And I can guarantee that there aren't very many duck hunters who will pass up the opportunity to take a honker! Doing so would be akin to ordering roast beef and throwing away the gravy!

But with the increase in goose populations a new phenomenon is occurring. We're seeing more and more hunters heading for the marshes, fields and waterways with a focus on goose hunting. And the ebbing ducks are often considered the gravy!

Though similar methods do work for taking ducks and geese, the hunter who goes afield with geese as the primary target will turn the odds in his favor if he throws some special twists on the old-standby waterfowling methods.

Some hunting of geese is done over water, but the majority is carried on in the fields where geese come to feed on leftover grain crops such as corn, wheat, rice and soybeans. Different decoys, calls and terrain are utilized in hunting the various goose species, but really they are only slight variations on the same theme.

Hunting Canadas: Field & Water
Field Hunting. There are three basic types of field hunting for geese: from fixed or semi-permanent blinds located prior to the sea-

son, locating favorite feeding fields each day and setting up in them with decoys, and lastly, sneaking up on feeding geese.

Permanent blinds are typically located before the season in feeding fields next to refuges or areas that have traditionally held geese from generation to generation. Geese have a strong tendency to come back to these areas year after year. Unless habitat changes are drastic, goose hunting will predictably be very good for many seasons.

Because of this, there are many commercial goose hunting operations offering leases for a day, week or month for those willing to pay. Some offer the very finest hunting, but some are shoddy operations with only "the buck" in mind. The latter will run hunters through a hot blind in shifts. After one group of hunters kills their limit from passing birds, another group is hauled out to the blind. It's definitely not a quality goose hunt.

Many of the field goose hunting situations on public land are not much better. The geese are usually extremely concentrated, but soon learn to fly well above shotgun range or avoid the blinds completely. All this often leads to skybusting and tremendous crippling problems.

In either case, the hunter is likely to find himself feeling like he's stuck with the problem. If he lucks out and both the geese and fellow hunters are cooperating, hunting can be good. But when everything fails to come together, which it usually does, the hunt will be dismal.

On the other hand, with the right set up and situation, hunting decoying geese in a prime feed field can be one of the most exciting and challenging forms of waterfowling. It takes proper blind location, a good number of quality decoys, and, most importantly, good calling! But there is no doubt *it is* exciting when half a hundred big old Canada honkers come drifting down to land in your spread while you sit a dozen yards away, hunkered in a pit blind.

You can quite often lease or rent land for goose blinds around most of the refuges or public hunting areas. The price can be extremely high, and you can quite often do better "free-lancing" for geese some distance away from the refuge. Naturally geese will use the feed fields close to the refuge during the first part of the season. As they gradually eat up the food, and as they continually get more hunting pressure from these areas, they will fly further and further from the refuge to find feeding fields.

Locating the feeding fields of these flocks, then asking permission from the landowner to hunt will often get a hearty go ahead! Geese can quickly destroy a winter wheat crop or vacuum up a corn

Decoying geese from large flocks can be difficult. Concentrate on singles, pairs and flocks up to 20-25.

patch in nothing flat, so many landowners who aren't as near the refuge generally will welcome the help in cutting down on goose populations. They aren't as liable to charge for hunting privileges either.

The best technique to locate feeding fields is to watch the early morning flights through binoculars, and follow with an automobile until the flight settles down to feed. Geese may fly 20 to 30 miles from the refuge to find what they are looking for. They may head back to the refuge mid-morning, or feed all day and fly back in late afternoon depending on weather, how much food is available and how far they have flown from the refuge.

Once you find a good feed field, ask permission to hunt either that afternoon or the following day. It's important to hunt the field as soon as possible after discovering it.

Set up as many high quality field decoys as you can lay your hands on including a combination of silhouettes, rags, full-bodies and windsocks. Windsocks, some type of full-bodies like the Farm-Form Decoy and even kites are important to the spread because they imitate natural movement that geese are used to seeing from the air.

Geese will not come near any kind of unusual obstacle in a field, and they generally prefer to feed in the center of a field rather than next to fencerows, etc.. You should choose your blind or shooting spot in accordance.

For instance don't set up in a hedge or next to a tree line, nor by a brush patch, etc.. Instead, pick the highest spot in the field and as close to the center as possible. Make sure all decoys are facing into the wind and in a natural feeding position. The majority of the decoys should have feeder heads with one or two upright heads for every dozen or so feeders.

The simplest blind, and one that works well especially in the early part of the season, is for hunters to lie on the ground and cover themselves with camouflage nets or cloth. If there is snow on the ground, an old sheet with holes cut in it works well, or you can use white camouflage clothing.

You can also help break up the pattern by covering hunters with pieces of natural camouflage such as corn stalks. From then on it's simply a matter of good calling. Make sure everyone lies perfectly still until the geese are in range, which usually means when they start to settle down into the decoys. Then, on the leader's command everyone should raise and fire in unison. It's guaranteed excitement!

Especially when hunting with a number of partners, it's best to discuss ahead of time assigned shooting zones and which bird in the flock each hunter will take on the initial volley. You'll increase your

One of goose hunting's greatest rewards is in taking a youngster hunting and teaching him the tricks of the trade.

bag from each flock and make for a safer hunt.

It does take a dedicated hunter to withstand the rigors of the hunt. You will often have to lie on the cold wet ground for a long time before you get any shooting action. Then the action happens quickly and close at hand. Stiffened muscles and frozen fingers do little to improve your wing shooting, not to mention that you'll take most of your shots from a sitting or kneeling position.

If a particular field promises to provide continued good hunting, you should seek further permission from the farmer to hunt and dig pit blinds. If you've acted responsibly and ethically during your time on his land, he'll probably grant you permission with the simple request that you fill in the pits by the end of the season.

When digging a mid-season pit, you should always carry away the soil you've excavated rather than throwing it aside in the field. The freshly turned soil can easily be discerned from the air, and spook wary geese. Once the pit is dug, you can cover the top with a light wire screen covered with material to match the surroundings.

A pincer-type sneak on feeding geese can result in great shooting for both the pushers and the standers.

Sneak Hunting Fields. Another method of hunting geese that are feeding in a field is to make a stalk or sneak on them. If you spot a flock feeding and get permission to set up for a later hunt, you might first make a sneak hunt on those birds.

Because geese are extremely wary, it takes a heck of a lot of patience, not to mention luck, to sneak up on a flock of feeding birds. As mentioned earlier, they will almost always feed away from obstacles that you might use to conceal your stalk. And there will always be one or more sentries on the highest ground watching for the smallest sign of danger. At the slightest hint, they will sound the alarm and the entire flock will flush immediately.

Crawling on your belly toward a flock of feeding geese, however, is excitement in the first degree. First, watch the flock to determine which direction they are feeding in a field. They move constantly, sort of leap frogging over each other, each family bunch trying to get the best food. If you can determine which direction they are headed and make your stalk from that direction, you will have the advantage of having them work their way towards your ambush.

Goose hunting can be a lot of frustrating work, but the rewards are in line with the size of the birds.

Again, if you're lucky enough to have snow on the ground, you can wear white camouflage to disappear into the terrain and increase your chances for a successful sneak. But even at that, 50 yards is about as close as you'll get regardless of how good you are at crawling on your belly through frozen, icy mud and water!

One situation where the sneak works particularly well is when geese are feeding in partially harvested corn fields. Hunters can use the remaining standing corn as cover to move as close to the geese as possible before using the belly crawl to close the final gap.

A pincer tactic using two hunters can increase the odds of sneaking up on geese. One hunter should position himself in any available cover, upwind of the flock. Try to determine the most logical flight path for escaping birds. He should try to get as close as possible to the birds without revealing himself.

The second hunter makes the stalk into the wind toward the geese. If the stalking hunter is successful in getting close to the geese, so much the better. He is liable to get some shooting and possibly down a goose or two.

But most of the operation's success relies on the crackshot hidden upwind in the weeds. Regardless of the stalker's success, when the geese spook they will fly directly into the wind and toward the waiting hunter. If all the conditions are right and the hidden hunter is in good position, he may be in the best of all waterfowling situations to take the elusive triple on web-footed birds!

Water Sets For Geese

Most geese taken over water sets are incidental to ducks. In areas with high concentrations of both ducks and geese, decoy spreads can be set for both at the same time and geese are often taken in that manner. The chapter on decoys explains how to make up the proper sets for this type of hunting. Again the biggest factor is having a large number of decoys and also the most lifelike you can afford.

Water sets will work quite well late in the season when the majority of the area is frozen and you.can provide open water as resting areas for the birds.

Geese like large bodies of open water and vast marshes both with grain fields close at hand. Good "over water" goose hunting sites have traditionally been the larger rivers, bays and flooded plains.

Hunting Snows And Blues

Snow and blue geese are hunted in basically the same way as Canada geese, with a few slight differences. Snows and blues gener-

On some days you'll swear that snow geese were born without brains, the next you'll never get a shot.

ally travel in much larger flocks and family groups than Canadas. They usually go out to feed about daylight and feed up until about 11:00 a.m.. Then just before sunset they may head back out to feed again. If the moon is full, they may feed all night long. They usually spend the middle of the day loafing and resting on mud flats, sand bars and other places with gravel for grit. Or they may spend the loafing hours on open water. In iced-over areas, they may actually sit on the ice. If they can find a winter wheat field, they will graze all day if not disturbed.

The best method of hunting snows and blues is to scout the country surrounding refuges or goose holding areas until you find their feeding fields. Do this during the evening feed flights, and don't disturb them that day. In fact, many areas like Manitoba, Canada are closed to waterfowl hunting after noon. Even in Texas, where it usually legal to hunt the afternoon flights, sportsmen have a "gentlemen's agreement" that you simply don't hunt birds on a roost pond. They feel this is the least the birds deserve and helps maintain good hunting throughout the season.

When you find a promising field and have secured permission to hunt it, plan to hunt the geese in the morning. You can set up decoys that night after dark (where it's legal to do so) or put them out before sunrise in the morning. If you set them up the night before a hunt in an area that has a chance of frost or dew, you may have to wipe the dekes dry in the morning so they won't shine in the rising sun.

The huge flocks that are common with snows and blues sometimes make calling the birds the biggest problem. These flocks may
number in the hundreds or thousands, and they probably just plain
can't hear you over the noise they make themselves! Smaller flocks
of 15 or 20 can usually be called quite easily.

Again, because of the size of the flocks it takes a lot of decoys to
bring in the birds. They will however decoy to almost anything that
is dull white. That's why rag hunting is popular with many snow
goose hunters. As mentioned in the chapter on decoys, these can be
most anything from commercially produced hunting rags to diapers
to white garbage bags. Anything white to light gray will work as
long as conditions are such that no shine will be thrown off the
decoys.

A good spread may consist of 200-300 rags plus another hundred
good full-body decoys. Bleach bottles or white plastic milk jugs
work, too. Some Texas hunting guides like Pat Johnson of the Wild
Goose Hunting Club in El Campo, Texas and Chuck Barry of Texas
Hunting Products, Houston, recommend 100-200 rags for each
hunter gunning from a spread.

Decoys are usually placed with a big main spread and then a
smaller spread set out separately and appearing to feed toward the
main group.

White parkas or coveralls are often worn by the hunters, who
simply lie down among the decoys. Then again, it's a matter of proper calling, and making sure every hunter lies perfectly still. Chuck
Barry says the beginning hunter's most common mistake is "head
bobbing"; that's picking your head off the ground because you just
have to watch the geese.

The scenario usually consists of a handful of geese dropping out
of the main flock and landing in the set, while the main flock continues to circle and circle and circle, frazzling the nerves of even the
most steel nerved hunter. Eventually a few more will land, and then
begins the "funnel" as the entire flock starts making ever smaller
circles to funnel down on top of the waiting hunters!

If you can stand it, you're going to have some exciting shooting!
Everyone rises at the command of a hunting leader and shoots, picking their shots carefully because of the closeness of hunters and
geese.

Quite often if you nail the lead geese the juveniles will continue
milling in the area providing chances for everyone to fill out a limit
of geese in one "fowl swoop."

One unusual factor in snow and blue goose behavior is that there may be some geese that visit a field in the morning and some that come in the afternoon. They'll do so with a regularity that is uncanny! You can practically set your watch by them. To be really successful, it's a good idea to watch a feed field for a couple of days to discern the best position to make your ambush.

Hunting Whitefronted Geese

Whitefronted geese, also called specklebellies often fly with other geese and are quite often taken in that manner. In fact, many hunter mix a few speck decoys in with their Canada and snow goose sets. A predominantly specklebelly set will also work work in areas where this species is concentrated.

Specks have basically the same feeding habits as Canada geese and are hunted in virtually the same manner. They are quite wary, however, and will usually circle and mill around the decoy spread for some time before committing themselves. Then they all come at once and make a high pitched laughing sound when they land among the decoys.

Flagging Geese

One method that is growing in use for both light goose and dark goose species is *flagging*. This consists of waving a white or black flag, depending on the species you're after, so geese at a distance will notice the movement and swing in for a closer look. It works well, especially on young birds that haven't seen the technique before.

Shooting Geese

Hunting geese is often the easy part, if you can believe it! Killing them is usually the hardest.

They are big birds, and usually appear to be much closer than they are. They also appear to fly much more slowly than they actually do.

The two most common mistakes that cause lost geese or cripples is shooting at the birds when they are too far away, and shooting behind them. The old story about pointing at the lead goose in a flock and taking the one behind it has a great deal of truth to it.

There are several things you can do to help prevent shooting at geese that are too far away. One method is to place a few stakes around your blind at about 40 yards. Geese within that circle should be within range unless they're a mile in the sky. Another method is to hold your fire until you can see their feet or eyes clearly. Then you will know the goose is in range for a clean kill.

To prevent shooting behind them, concentrate on keeping a good lead, remember they are flying faster than they appear. Aim for the head, and pretend you are killing a quail or busting a clay bird, which are both about the size of a goose's head. You'll be surprised how quickly your percentage on geese will improve!

Weather Influences

Hunting geese is usually at its worst during a full moon when the geese won't start out to feed until late in the evening. Then, they feed all night and return to the safety of the refuge to loaf all day before repeating the process.

The best time to hunt geese is on cold, windy days just ahead of a leading storm front or those with some fog or mist. In both cases, geese will move all day.

Things To Remember

Regardless of which species of goose you're after, there are a couple simple rules that can increase your chances for success.

As long as the geese are coming toward you don't call, don't move, and, above all, *don't shoot unless they are settling in the decoys.*

13

Brant, Sea Ducks And Other Waterfowl

In addition to the more common waterfowl mentioned in the identification chapter, as well as elsewhere in this book, there are a number of other migratory waterbirds that are hunted as well. Some, like the coot, are well-known to waterfowlers across the country. Others, like the clapper rail and scoter, are quite limited in their distribution, and hunting opportunities for them are not widespread.

Some of these other birds are considered waterfowl, while others are marsh or shore birds. They are all mentioned in this book because they can afford the wise hunter some interesting time afield even if the more popular species aren't cooperating.

Like most migratory birds, the populations of these species fluctuate with changing weather and habitat conditions, and with natural cycles that we still don't fully understand. Not all of them are as numerous today as in the famed market hunting days, but they all offer unique challenges for hunters who want to keep their shotgun barrels warm when other species aren't flying.

Brant

Brant shooting has long been a tradition with waterfowlers on both coasts. The American Brant is found along the Atlantic Coast, while the Black Brant is found along the Pacific Coast.

Quite similar to a small Canada goose, the brant is a small, darkly colored bird. It has a dark chest and belly instead of the light col-

Hunters who want to be in on the action will turn to other species of waterfowl and shorebirds when the ducks and geese aren't cooperating.

Brant

ored belly of the Canada goose. They also have a small white neck ring, but it is difficult to see in flight.

Brant are primarily birds of the coastal saltwater bays, lagoons and tidal flats. They spend the majority of their time in the open water, coming into the shallows to feed on eel grass and sea lettuce, their most common foods. They fly fairly rapidly, staying low to the water and making a soft *"ker-honking"* sound.

Atlantic Brant numbers have fluctuated greatly in the last century. The decline in the amount of eel grass and the vagaries of the weather on their arctic breeding grounds are the two main reasons.

Black Brant numbers have been more stable. Except for 1959, their numbers have remained more than 100,000 birds.

Brant are typically hunted over decoys much in the same manner as geese and ducks. Some hunters set up on traditional feeding grounds using floating blinds and large rafts of decoys. Others watch for daily feeding patterns, and set up shore blinds on shoreline points or islands near those areas.

There are a variety of Federal Regulations governing the hunting of brant, and they tend to vary from year to year. Be sure you understand the constraints before you hunt these magnificent birds.

Sea Ducks

Oldsquaw. One of the most colorful sea ducks, the oldsquaw is

Old Squaw

found on both coasts and on the Great Lakes. Their distinctive black and white pattern and long sweeping tail are good marks to look for in the field. Their wing patch is light brown.

Oldsquaws are fast flying ducks which usually stay fairly low over the water and form irregular, loose flocks that fly as one unit. They are extremely vocal, making a loud whistling sound.

Harlequin Ducks. Also found on both coasts, the harlequin is one of the most bizzarely colored waterfowl anywhere. The drake is slate blue with brown sides and an array of white dashes and spots on its head, neck and scapulas. The hen is brown, with a light colored chest and three white spots on the head. They resemble closely the female bufflehead, but are larger and show no white patches in flight.

Harlequins are occasionally found on mountain streams. They

swim with a bobby motion and are often found with scoters. They are usually silent.

Scoters. Scoters are fairly common sea ducks that concentrate in bays along the coasts. They eat primarily animal life, with clams being their preferred food.

There are three species of scoters: the *black* or *common* scoter, which is the smallest; the *surf* scoter, which is the next largest; and the *white-winged* scoter, which is the largest.

Scoters fly in an irregular, wavering line and stay close to the water's surface. They all appear black from a distance, but the white wings that give the largest birds their name set them apart from the others.

Harlequin Ducks

Whitewing Scoter. Surf Scoter. Common Scoter.

Scoters are birds of the icy seas and can be found as far north as the Arctic Ocean. They are mostly silent.

Eiders. There are several different species of eiders. They include the *common*, found in the coastal regions of the arctic; the *king*, in the North Arctic, the North Atlantic and Pacific coasts; the *Steller's*, found along the coast of Alaska; and the *spectacled*, one of the rarest North American ducks.

Eiders, with the exception of the Steller's, are some of the largest ducks in North America. The common eider weighs up to six pounds and the king eider nearly four.

They usually fly low to the water, sometimes even in the trough of a wave. They are stocky, thick-necked birds that appear ungainly in flight.

The distinctive shape of all eiders and their unique colorings are unmistakable. They are usually silent.

Coots

Mention coots to many waterfowlers and you'll get a hearty laugh. Too bad. Coot are good eating and can provide a lot of shooting fun.

One of the reasons they are less than attractive to some hunters is because of their other names: *mudhen, rice hen, marsh hen.*

Coot

They are slow to startle, and must patter along the surface of the water for some distance before taking off.

Coot don't decoy well, so you have to jumpshoot them or find a good pass shooting sight. They can be somewhat easy to bag, but for a challenge, try pass shooting them on a windy day. I guarantee a lot of empty hulls in the bottom of the boat for the number of birds you bag.

Coots are found over most of North America, and most states have generous bag limits since few hunters try for them. Most coot are quite trusting because of a lack of hunting pressure.

Coots can dive quite easily and will often do so after being shot. Make sure you dispatch cripples immediately or they will dive underwater and hang on to vegetation. They are primarily vegetarian and if dressed and cooked properly, can provide some excellent tablefare. Check chapter 14 for some recipes I highly recommend.

Jacksnipe

One of the most opportunistic migratory marsh bird hunting situations is for jacksnipe. They can be found scattered over most of North America during their fall migrations. They concentrate, however, in the South and Southeast during the winter. There are also good populations that winter along the West Coast as well.

Though they resemble woodcock in many ways, the jacksnipe is a more slender bird. They have long bills and small bodies like timberdoodles, but their heads are striped, not barred like the woodcock's. They fly in a zipping, circling, zig-zagging flight that makes them extremely difficult to hit.

Also called *common snipe* or simply *snipe*, they are found around swamps and boggy areas. They are quite often taken as a bonus bird by waterfowlers moving to or from their blinds or sneak hunting mallards in marshes. In states like Florida or Louisiana, however, many hunters hit the marshes with nothing but snipe on their minds.

Rails

There are four different kinds of rails hunted in North America: the *clapper rail*, which is found in coastal marshlands; the *king rail*, found in much of the eastern United States; and the *Virginia* and *Sora* rails found in most freshwater marshes across the country.

Rails, like snipe, are taken mostly by opportunistic waterfowlers. In the Southeast, however, many hunters pursue rails exclusively by wading through shallow marshes or poling through

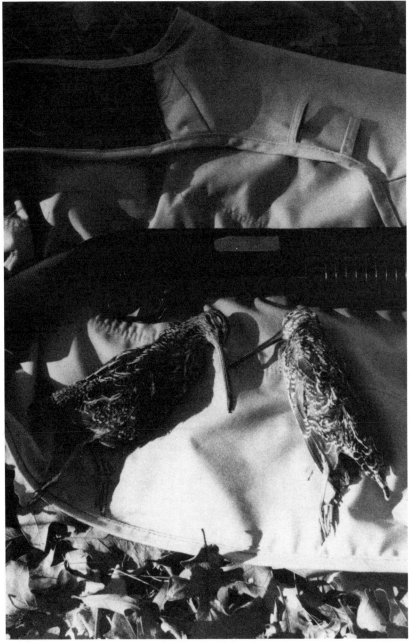

Jacksnipe are most often a target of opportunity for waterfowl hunters, but they are fun hunting in their own right.

tall marsh grass or cattails. The larger king and clapper rails can run and dive very well. They are almost as large as small ducks!

The smaller inland rails are more likely to flush than the larger birds. They weave and twist when they fly, and are very difficult to hit.

For the table, rails are prepared the same as snipe.

Whistling Swans

The large size and the all white plumage of the adult whistling swan makes it easy to distinguish them from the snow goose. Down to 49,000 birds in 1950, the whistling swan's numbers have been slowly increasing since then. Some states now have seasons on them, though hunting is very limited.

Whistling swans feed largely on leaves, stems and tubers of aquatic plants. Their extremely long necks allow them to feed without tipping like puddle ducks. They have been known to eat waste corn in some areas as well.

Sandhill Cranes

Once nearly extinct, sandhill crane populations are coming back very strongly. They are found throughout much of the Mississippi, Central and Pacific flyways as well as in Florida and Georgia.

Hunting is generally limited and by permit only, but seasons are open and restrictions are relaxed in more states each season.

14

Cleaning Ducks and Geese

When it comes to the pursuit of waterfowl, hunting is the enjoyable part; cleaning is the chore. Of all game, waterfowl is probably the most time consuming, and in some ways the most difficult of all game to prepare for the table.

Regardless, no game should ever be wasted. Even the less revered species of waterfowl can provide good eating if some special care is taken with their dressing and table preparation.

Dressing

There are several different methods of cleaning ducks and geese, depending on the species, the cooking method you intend to use on that particular bird, how much time you have, the facilities and equipment you have available, etc. Some methods take only a minute or two, others may take almost an hour for a big bird.

Dry Plucking. The most common method of dressing is to dry pluck the bird. This can be done by hand or with any number of special duck pickers. The motorized duck pickers can speed up the chore a great deal, but regardless, it is a messy, and time consuming job. You might as well sit down and make yourself comfortable.

Use a large grocery or paper sack to pluck over and to help contain the feathers and down. If you intend to save the down keep it separate from the main feathers.

There are several "tricks" to make dry plucking easier. The first

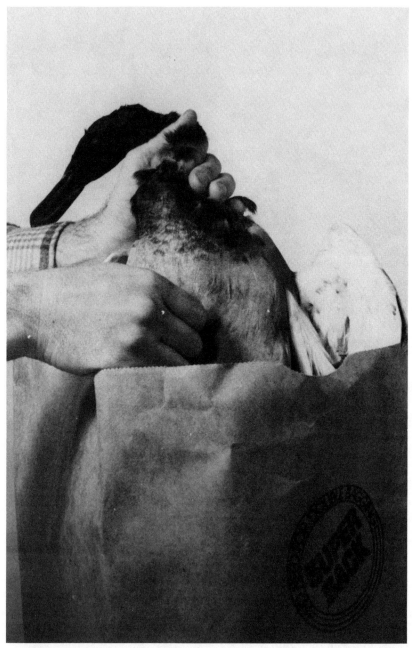

Dry pluck ducks over a paper bag. Pluck downward with the lay of the feathers. Pluck ducks as soon as possible after taking them.

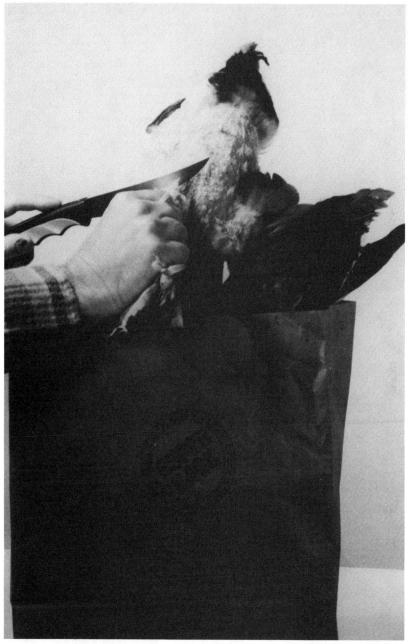

After removing the feathers and down, cut off the wings by twisting in the socket and cutting loose the large muscle.

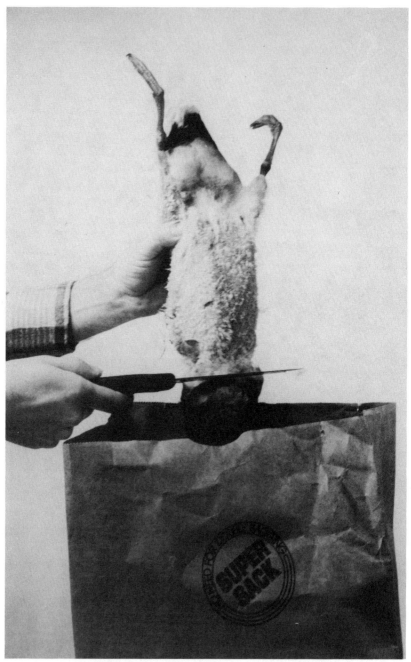

Use a sharp knife to remove the head.

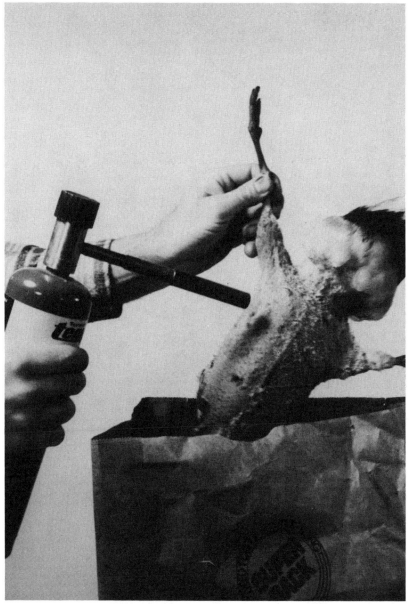

A shop blow torch can be used to scorch off tiny hairs, pieces of down, etc.

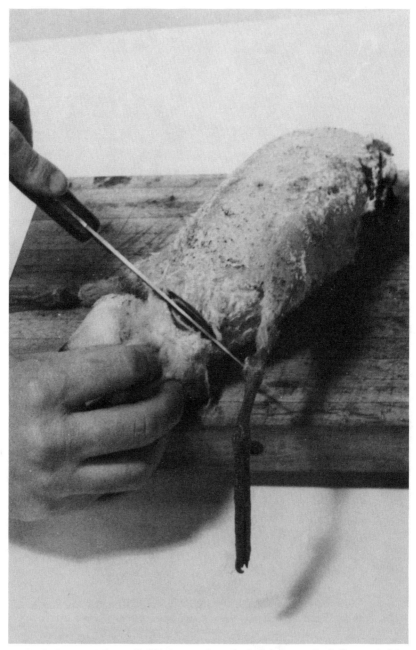

On birds that are to be stuffed and roasted, make a slice across the belly, around the tail to remove entrails and tail at one time.

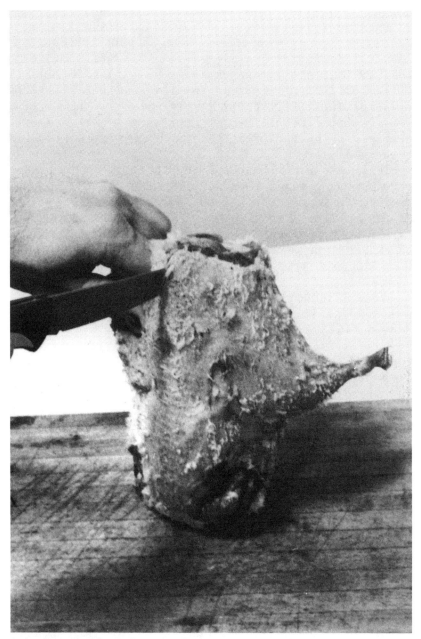

A simpler method for ducks is to remove the tail, then stand the carcass on either end and slice down both sides of the backbone, removing backbone and entrails at one time.

is to pick the birds as soon as possible after they are killed. The feathers and down will release more easily then, and the skin doesn't tear quite as easily as it does after the bird has hung for some time. Another trick that simplifies picking is to pick downward, or toward the tail as the feathers will also release more easily in that direction.

Paraffin Dipping. One method used by some hunters is to pour melted paraffin in a bucket of hot water, and dip the ducks in that. Wrap the dipped ducks in newspaper, and allow the paraffin to cool. Then peel off the newspaper, paraffin, feathers and down, all in large chunks.

If using the paraffin method, remove the wings first to allow the paraffin to get in around all the body of the duck. When dry picking, leave the wings on for ease of handling the bird.

Pin Feathers. Once the majority of feathers and down are removed, it's time to remove the pin feathers. These are the small, dark shafts starting new feathers. They can be removed by pinching them with your fingers, or between the index finger and the blade of a knife.

You can further clean the bird after removing the pin feathers by using a torch to singe off the small "hair" feathers and tiny bits of down that may be adhered to the bird.

Cutting & Eviscerating

Next cut off the head. Cut around the wing socket with a sharp knife, bend the wing bone out of its socket and twist it off. You will probably have to cut some additional muscles to release the wing. Cut off the feet as well.

How the bird will be cooked determines how it will be gutted and cut up. There are several different methods that can be used. Usually ducks and geese are cleaned somewhat differently, because they are quite often cooked differently.

Ducks. There are, of course, several different ways to prepare ducks. If the birds are to be stuffed, or prepared whole, they are gutted by making a slice across the belly just below the rib cage. Slice down around the tail and remove the entrails and tail section at one time. Make sure the windpipe is pulled from the neck opening of the bird as well.

A method that is simpler, less messy and allows the birds to cook more thoroughly if they are not to be stuffed is to stand the bird on the base of its tail, and cut down through the ribs, along the back bone and each side of the neck. Do this on both sides of the backbone, then pull out the backbone, neck and entrails at one time.

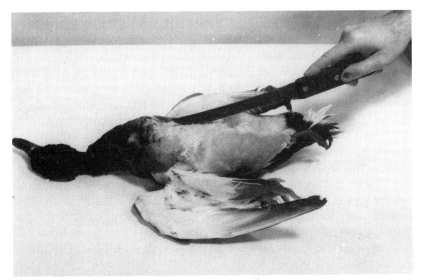

To remove the breast meat from a duck, pluck feathers and down from the breast area. Using a boning knife, slice down against the breast bone and turn the knife outward, following the curve of the bone. Cut away from the wing muscle and remove the skin.

Once the birds are eviscerated, wash out the cavity. Soak the birds overnight in a pan of cold salt water to help remove excess blood. One thing you must do regardless of all else is make sure you cut away any bloody areas or damaged flesh. Remove shot pellets from under the skin and muscle as well.

Geese. Since geese are usually roasted whole, and often times stuffed, they are usually cleaned by slicing across the belly, and down to the tail. Cut around the base of the tail to remove it and the entrails at the same time. Again, make sure the windpipe and crop are removed. Wash out the cavity, and make sure the lungs have been removed from the cavities on both sides of the backbone. You may also wish to soak the bird overnight in salt water, though some cooks feel this tends to dehydrate the meat.

Debreasting

One of the simplest and quickest methods of dressing ducks is debreasting. This is particularly useful on small ducks such as teal, and some divers. It only takes a few minutes, and you have most of the meat from these small birds.

The first step is to pull the feathers and down from the breast area. Then slice down on one side of the breast bone using a boning or fillet knife. Allow the knife to slide down the breast done to the side, and then peel the breast out. Cut it off at the wing joint, and remove the skin. Soak and clean as you usually would.

One thing about debreasting is that if you arrive home after a late day afield only to find you forgot about the party you promised your spouse you would go to, you can place the ducks in a paper bag in the freezer, and debreast them at the time you desire to cook them. They are as easily debreasted then as when freshly killed.

Saving the Down

Ducks and geese were important to early hunters not only for their excellent meat, but also to provide down for pillows, mattresses and clothing. Today, down can be used for those same purposes, although it rarely is. If you wish to save the down from your waterfowl it can easily be used to make your own down clothing or bedding.

Down to be used for those purposes must be cleaned of both the dirt and debris it collects, as well as lice and other "creepy crawlies." The simplest way of doing this is to place the down in cloth bags and hang it outside through the winter months. The sun, wind and rain will cleanse it thoroughly.

15

Hunting Waterfowl On Public Lands

Through the years past, a great deal of waterfowl hunting was done on private lands. Duck clubs like the late Jimmy Robinson's Sports Afield Duck Club on Manitoba's Delta Marsh and Nash Buckingham's beloved Beaver Dam were extremely popular among serious duck hunters. And though duck clubs are still popular with duck hunters across the country today, more and more duck hunting is done on public waterfowling lands. There are many such areas scattered around the country, and more are being added as funds become available. Most hunters today are within an hour's drive of some public waterfowling spot.

There are many good points that can be said about public waterfowling grounds, but there are some negative ones too. One of the advantages is low cost. Most public lands are open to hunters for free or at very reasonable cost. Another advantage is the large number of birds these areas draw. It is nothing for goose hunters along the Lac qui Parle Refuge area in western Minnesota to see upwards of 2,000 to 5,000 geese during a day's hunt. The trick in such areas is to be in the right place at the right time.

Of course, there are disadvantages associated with hunting on public grounds. One of the biggest is competition. Many waterfowlers flock to such areas, and often have to set up too close to each other. This often leads to skybusting, arguments and even fights. Game management personnel combat this problem in many

To be successful on public land where competition for ducks is stiff, a waterfowler must possess the best equipment and hunting skills. He'll also plan the time and place of his hunt to minimize competition from other hunters.

areas by holding lottery drawings for blinds before each morning's hunt.

Another disadvantage is the wariness of the birds in heavily hunted areas. By the middle of the season, the chances of success drop considerably. It seems the local waterfowl and those that move in with the first fall flights, become knowledgeable about blind locations and legal shooting times. They leave the refuges well before dawn to feed in areas many miles away, then come back late in the evening. That way they avoid hunting pressure almost entirely.

These birds also become very wise to refuge boundaries and heavily hunted areas. More than one hunter has told the tale of flight after flight of ducks and geese hugging the tops of the cattails until they were within 100 yards of the refuge's edge. Then they seemed to climb straight into the sky like rockets until they were well out of shotgun range before hitting the edge of the safe haven.

Sometimes this changes later in the season, however, when a number of "uneducated" ducks and geese are forced into these areas by a solid freeze to the north. These birds are very susceptible to hunters in blinds along refuge borders, but they too learn quickly.

Hunting these areas can provide some great shooting for those willing to make the proper preparations and work for it. The best success is usually on the very first weekend or week of the season. The next best is the last third of the season.

The open-water marsh areas provide the most challenge—and problems—in public waterfowl hunting. Field situations are next. Flooded timber public hunting areas usually provide a quality hunt. Many areas have separate flooded timber areas set aside for "walk-in" hunters. These areas are usually limited to a specific number of hunters each day. The hunting is usually of a higher quality, though more work, than using fixed blinds in marsh or field.

Timing The Public Land Hunt

Timing is often quite important in hunting public areas. On private hunting areas, the best hunting occurs in the first few hours of the morning. On public hunting land, however, the best hunting quite often occurs from about 10 o'clock in the morning to the middle of the afternoon. It's not unusual for the first early morning flights to be high and extremely early. About 10 o'clock the birds start drifting back in small groups. These are "working birds" that can usually be called much easier. By that time, however, most hunters have left in frustration.

Boosting Your Chances On Public Land

There are things you can do to help your chances of success in public hunting areas. The first is to thoroughly police the area around your blind and pick up all the debris you find. After the first week or so of the season some blinds begin to look more like a dump than a duck blind. Pick up empty shotshells, cigarette packs and candy wrappers, etc.; from the air they stand out like beacons, alerting already wary waterfowl of your presence.

The second thing you can do is to take along some extra vegetation or camouflage material to refurbish the blind for your hunt. In many instances you won't be able to cut native material for the blind. Camouflage cloth works well if vegetation is not available. Use it to cover everything around the blind, especially shiny things like aluminum boats and thermos bottles. Refuge birds are very blind wary, so take the time to cover everything completely.

On public land, the key to success lies in doing what the other guys aren't. For example, if they're all after mallards, you concentrate on another species.

Wearing a face net or camouflage makeup is another thing you can do to help assure success. It's odd that more waterfowl hunters don't think of this. A face shining up out of the blind is very visible to passing birds. You will be surprised at the different way birds react to your set-up with this one change.

Of course, good calling is also very important when hunting public areas. Bill Harper, an excellent caller, has one thing to say about calling ducks on public hunting areas. "Most hunters call way too much." In Bill's estimation some of the old mallards on some public hunting areas can not only tell what brand of call a hunter is using, but the model number as well.

There is a smattering of truth to that. If you've ever listened to the calls in a public hunting area, it's a symphony of highballs, with an odd call thrown in. Keep your calling to a minimum.

Bill's suggestion is extremely important for working refuge birds. Call only when birds are undecided or working away from you. Never call when they're coming into your set. The only exception to this is perhaps, a few low feeding chuckles or a soft quack or two such as made by contented, feeding ducks.

In many heavily used and regulated areas, decoys are sometimes available for rent. They are often permanently placed near blinds or pits at regular intervals. If you were to fly over the area you would quite often see two to three dozen decoys, no more or no less, all looking exactly alike. It's a repetitious pattern that often spooks already wary ducks and geese.

Some hunters have found that taking some of their own decoys, or simply taking ones that are different than the rented decoys, can provide more success. Use as realistic a decoy as possible and set them properly. Placing your decoys where ducks or geese want to land and providing landing areas for them, is more important than how many decoys you have in these heavily hunted areas. However, in areas with big flocks of birds, you will need huge sets to compete. This is especially true for geese.

When setting out your decoys, make sure the ones on the outside of your landing area are no more than 45 yards from your blind or shooting position. This helps you know when ducks or geese are in good killing range, thereby reducing the possibility of cripples.

Confidence decoys can also provide more success on public hunting areas, but few hunters use them. That's a mistake. A couple of Canada goose decoys or a fake gull or heron placed near the blind can often help sway wary ducks. Choose confidence decoys that replicate species common to your hunting area.

There are literally thousands of public hunting areas scattered across the United States. They range from tiny potholes off the beaten track to world-famous areas such as the huge Bayou Meto Duck Hunting Area near Stuttgart, Arkansas, or the famous Swan Lake area in Missouri.

There is also a lot of difference in the type of hunting available in these areas. It ranges from marsh to flooded green timber, open bays, cypress swamps and big lakes. The rules and regulations vary quite a bit as well. Some of the more popular areas have fairly strict rules and many require advance reservations. In some cases, where demand for blinds is extremely high, there may even be a random drawing of advance reservation cards for blinds. Other areas are on a first-come, first-serve basis.

Choosing The Right Area

The first step is to decide where you want to hunt then contact your fish and game department or the one in the state you plan to hunt and request a listing of public waterfowling areas. If possible get maps of the areas as well as specific regulations. Then you may wish to contact one of the managers of the area for specifics such as the results of last year's season, etc., and go from there.

Etiquette

Though sportsmanship and hunting ethics are important no matter where you are hunting, they are never more so than on crowded public hunting areas. Just use common sense and don't let yourself get carried away by the excitement of the moment.

Be gracious enough to accept the fact that somebody got up earlier than you did and got the best spot. Don't crowd hunters who are already set up. Be in position before shooting time arrives, that way you won't spoil opportunities for others by stumbling in during prime shooting times.

Keep your dog under control at all times. Allow for the fact that the guy down the row may have hit the bird you thought you did. Practice safe firearms handling techniques. *And above all don't shoot at birds that are out of range!*

There is no place in waterfowling today for a "you can't hit 'em if you don't shoot at them" attitude. Skybusters have probably ruined more waterfowl hunts on public land for more people than any other cause. They ruin a hunt just as surely as an anti-hunting saboteur, and you have every right to let them know what you think about their practices.

16

The Future of Waterfowling

What is the future of waterfowling? Will our sons and daughters and their children enjoy the thrilling sight of big mallard greenheads side-slipping down to their decoys? Will they tremble excitedly as 50 huge Canada honkers hover just over their heads, deciding whether or not to come into a set of decoys on the frozen ground of a corn field? Will they curse their cold, numb fingers as they fumble to get more shells out of their pocket after two straight misses on a buzzing flight of bluebills?

It's anybody's guess as to the long range future of waterfowl, or for that matter, most wildlife. Waterfowl, however, have special problems. It's relatively easy for wildlife managers to control and maintain populations of game such as quail, deer and turkeys because these species are basically "homebodies." By regulating the harvest in a particular area and increasing the quality of the habitat, the flock or herd can be managed and numbers increased, or decreased as needed to keep a stable, healthy population of wildlife.

Waterfowl on the other hand, often enter, live in and vacate three countries in the cycle of their annual migrations. Most species are found nesting in Canada, migrating through the United States and wintering in Mexico. Some species will nest and winter in the U.S., however, and some nest and winter both in the South.

Waterfowl numbers rarely remain constant. Like the stock market, they tend to follow a boom and bust cycle.

The 1950s were good for waterfowl, we had the largest number of birds in modern history, and hunting was very good. The bottom fell out during the 1960s, and waterfowl numbers dropped drastically. And the 80s have been even worse. In fact, a 1984 survey showed the lowest population levels of many species of waterfowl since records have been kept. Most waterfowl biologists as well as hunters, are worried and rightly so.

There are many problems waterfowl face, but the single biggest one is loss of habitat. There is a steady erosion of wetlands that doesn't appear to be slowing down. Duck-producing potholes in Canada and the United States are being cleared for agriculture, rivers and creeks are flooded for reservoirs, and sloughs and marshes are being drained for land development. It won't be long before good places for ducks and geese to nest and live will cease to exist.

Though you can manage some other wildlife in small, isolated places, waterfowl need lots of room to live and multiply. Without it, populations of waterfowl are simply going to decrease. The matter is that black and white.

The most tragic loss of habitat is in the prime nesting areas of North America. Sixty-five percent or more of the waterfowl in North America nest in the pothole regions of Canada. Traditionally, conditions of those regions have the greatest influence on most waterfowl populations.

If there is a spring through summer drought, or worse yet a series of dry years, there is a large decline in the population of many waterfowl species simply because they have no place to nest. Mallards, pintails and other puddle duck species are usually the hardest hit when such conditions occur.

One of the biggest problems facing nesting waterfowl in the pothole regions of both Canada and the U.S. these days is the continued loss of nesting habitat through the draining of potholes and marshes to gain grain-producing land. This will probably continue to be an increasing problem, as more and more farmers attempt to increase their productive acreage to keep up with rising costs and dropping prices for their products. Like the market hunting era of bygone days, it is an unfortunate case of economics taking precedent over ducks.

With the knowledge that loss of habitat is the biggest problem waterfowl faces today and in the future, the big questions all waterfowl hunters must ask: "What is being done about it? And what can be done about it?"

The answers are in group and individual conservation efforts.

What is the future of waterfowling? Will our children get to experience the same thrilling moments we did? (Photo courtesy of USFWS.)

Ducks Unlimited

The answer to both questions comes from several different sources. Probably the single biggest spokesgroup to prevent the loss of habitat is Ducks Unlimited. This organization of more than half a million concerned sportsmen and conservationists has raised over $337 million for waterfowl habitat since its start back in 1937. The money has been used to fund 2,794 wetland projects for waterfowl. These projects encompass a total of 1,700,000 acres, and DU has another 1.5 million acres that are earmarked for future projects. Over the next 15 years, DU will attempt to commit $585 million to North American waterfowl conservation.

Ducks Unlimited projects were started in the Prairie Provinces of Saskatchewan, Manitoba and Alberta, Canada when a severe drought threatened the traditional prairie nesting grounds of North American waterfowl. Since that start, DU has expanded their projects into British Columbia, Ontario, Mexico and some of the northern states, including Alaska. Much of the work in the United States has been done on already existing federal and state lands that needed funding assistance to continue and upgrade their habitat preservation and restoration efforts.

funding assistance to continue and upgrade their habitat preservation and restoration efforts.

There are also a number of other national and state waterfowling associations that lobby for prevention of wetland drainage and provide funds for habitat and wetlands conservation and restoration.

One of the most important things hunters can do to insure waterfowling for the future is to strongly support Ducks Unlimited and those local and national conservation associations dedicated to preserving wetlands and habitat for waterfowl.

Individual states, as well as the Federal government, are also involved in preventing the loss of wetlands. Many have wildlife management and refuge areas scattered within their borders. Concerned sportsmen should keep a close watch on local and federal politics governing these areas and make sure the interests of waterfowl are being attended to. Remember, in the long run what's good for ducks is good for duck hunters.

Duck Stamps

One of the most popular and known conservation acts is the use of the Federal Duck Stamp to provide funds for wetland preservation, purchase and management. In the United States there are over 300 federal wildlife refuges, encompassing almost 30 million acres scattered across the United States. They offer protection for waterfowl and many other forms of wildlife. In addition, the individual states have over seven million acres of wetlands that they manage primarily for waterfowl, using the money from state duck stamps. Every time a hunter purchases a waterfowling stamp, federal or state, he is helping to preserve the resource and the sport.

Lead Shot/Steel Shot

Until recently, the majority of modern shotshell ammunition used for waterfowl hunting has contained lead pellets. The properties of lead made it the most dependable and economical material to use in shotgun shells.

Through the decades of hunters pursuing their livelihood, then their sport in heavily hunted areas, there was a build up of spent lead shot accumulating in marsh muck and on lake bottoms. Many of these areas are, of course, prime waterfowl feeding areas!

Unfortunately, many waterfowl picked up lead shot when feeding, and over the years millions of ducks have died of lead poisoning because they ingested these spent lead pellets. The lead shot has also been shown to be a second-hand killer of many predatory birds like eagles and osprey, which feed on the dead or dying waterfowl.

Because of this, the Fish and Wildlife Service, in 1976, began requiring hunters to use nontoxic steel shot in certain designated zones where lead poisoning was a problem.

Over the years a number of techniques have been used to identify lead poisoning problem areas. In 1976, the Service's final environmental impact statement on the use of steel shot stated that nontoxic shot zones would be determined on the basis of the magnitude of waterfowl harvest, the density of deposited shot, the incidence of shot in waterfowl gizzards, measurements of lead levels in wing bones, visible evidence of mortality, and enforcement considerations in establishing easily identifiable boundaries, as well as other appropriate factors.

More recently, the Service has also considered the occurrence of lead in the soft tissue of waterfowl, such as liver and kidney, and measurements of blood enzyme levels indicating lead ingestion.

These techniques have been used individually or in combinations in various parts of the country. No single technique or combination of techniques was generally accepted by all federal and state authorities involved in designating nontoxic shot zones. As a result, the zones were not been established in a uniform manner throughout the country. Regional inequities in the application of nontoxic shot requirements for waterfowl hunting were commonplace.

Finally, 10 years after the nontoxic shot issue was raised, an equitable solution was achieved. In 1986, the USFWS laid down a frame work that requires the use of nontoxic shot for all waterfowl hunting in the United States beginning with the 1991 hunting season. This program, though still controversial, allows for a five year phase in to acclimate hunters and guarantee readily available supplies of nontoxic shot for all areas of the country.

Through all the intervening years, there has been a great deal of controversy concerning the use of steel shot, its effectiveness and whether it causes more problems than it cures, etc. Regardless, as of opening day 1991 all waterfowl hunters are using steel shot and fewer of our precious birds will be dying from lead poisoning!

Disease

Another serious problem that waterfowl managers face is a variety of diseases such as cholera and botulism, that attack various waterfowl. Many of these can be attributed to the overcrowding of waterfowl populations in some refuge areas. In many of these cases, lit-

If conservation efforts are to be successful, then every waterfowl hunter must come to take as much thrill in this sight as in a flock of greenheads pitching into the decoys. (Photo courtesy of USFWS.)

tle can be done to prevent the spread of disease. Most waterfowl dispersal attempts end in failure, or at best are a temporary solution to a long term problem.

Fortunately, research continues on avian diseases and their prevention in wild populations of waterfowl. Some day, there may be a solution to this problem, too.

The Individual Sportsman

There are many other things that individual hunters can do in addition to supporting conservation groups, purchasing waterfowling stamps and supporting legislation that favors wetland preservation and management.

The most important is to become a good hunter. This means learning to identify birds properly so high-point birds can be left alone. It also means becoming a good shot so the number of cripples are kept to a minimum, and using a retriever to help cut down on losses. It means being a conscientious hunter, and not always attempting to take the fullest limit possible. It means picking out low-point birds from a flock, and limiting your kill instead of killing your limit!

All of this shouldn't be looked upon as a dismal picture of the future of waterfowling. As more people, both hunters and non-hunters, become interested in waterfowl conservation, and learn the beauty of the marshes and waters as well as the challenge and excitement, there will be more effort to preserve this precious and traditional form of hunting for future generations. Our job as conscientious and responsible sportspersons is to make that happen!

Index